THE A–Z OF STUDENT WELLBEING

JAMIE O'DOWD
SERIES EDITOR: ROY BLATCHFORD

Together we unlock every learner's unique potential

At Hachette Learning (formerly Hodder Education), there's one thing we're certain about. No two students learn the same way. That's why our approach to teaching begins by recognising the needs of individuals first.

Our mission is to allow every learner to fulfil their unique potential by empowering those who teach them. From our expert teaching and learning resources to our digital educational tools that make learning easier and more accessible for all, we provide solutions designed to maximise the impact of learning for every teacher, parent and student.

Aligned to our parent company, Hachette Livre, founded in 1826, we pride ourselves on being a learning solutions provider with a global footprint.

www.hachettelearning.com

Although every effort has been made to ensure that website addresses are correct at time of going to press, Hachette Learning cannot be held responsible for the content of any website mentioned in this book. It is sometimes possible to find a relocated web page by typing in the address of the home page for a website in the URL window of your browser.

Hachette UK's policy is to use papers that are natural, renewable and recyclable products and made from wood grown in well-managed forests and other controlled sources. The logging and manufacturing processes are expected to conform to the environmental regulations of the country of origin.

To order, please visit www.HachetteLearning.com or contact Customer Service at education@hachette.co.uk / +44 (0)1235 827827.

ISBN: 978 1 0360 0731 7

© Jamie O'Dowd 2025

First published in 2025 by
Hachette Learning,
An Hachette UK Company
Carmelite House
50 Victoria Embankment
London EC4Y 0DZ
www.HachetteLearning.com

The authorised representative in the EEA is Hachette Ireland, 8 Castlecourt Centre, Dublin 15, D15 XTP3, Ireland (email: info@hbgi.ie)

Impression number   10 9 8 7 6 5 4 3 2 1
Year   2029 2028 2027 2026 2025

All rights reserved. Apart from any use permitted under UK copyright law, no part of this publication may be reproduced or transmitted in any form or by any means, electronic or mechanical, including photocopying and recording, or held within any information storage and retrieval system, without permission in writing from the publisher or under licence from the Copyright Licensing Agency Limited. Further details of such licences (for reprographic reproduction) may be obtained from the Copyright Licensing Agency Limited, www.cla.co.uk

Illustrations by DC Graphic Design Limited, Hextable, Kent.
Typeset in the UK.
Printed in the UK.
A catalogue record for this title is available from the British Library.

ACKNOWLEDGEMENTS

I would like to thank the outstanding school leaders I have been fortunate enough to work with during the last twenty years; Andrew Stephen, Nick Wilson, Ed Goodwin, Yasmine Dannawy and Simon Watson for giving me the time, confidence, belief, support and resources to develop my passion and interest in the leadership of wellbeing. To Mrs Fearn and Miss Lewis for caring about kids like me and for making me want to be 'that' teacher.

Thank you to the wonderful students of St Christopher's School who make it all worthwhile.

And most importantly, to Marie, Macie and Alfie. Love is all you need.

Jamie O'Dowd

CONTENTS

About the author v

Foreword by Roy Blatchford vi

Section One

Atmosphere 3

Behaviour 9

Character 17

Domino 23

Engagement 29

Flourishing 35

Gratitude 41

Happiness 49

Illbeing 55

Jenga 61

Knowledge 67

Language 73

Meaning 79

Nurturing 85

Openness 91

PERMA 99

Questioning 105

Restorative 111

Safeguarding 117

Thriving 121

Understanding 127

Voice 135

Welcomes 141

Xercising 147

You 153

Zzz 161

Section Two

1. Mapping/visualising wellbeing interventions: the speedometer 169

2. Digital leadership framework 171

3. Auditing your stakeholders 173

4. Example language charter 175

5. Enrichment/RSE 'roadmap' 177

6. Safeguarding legislation and policy 179

7. Mindfulness script 181

8. References 183

ABOUT THE AUTHOR

Jamie O'Dowd is Assistant Head at St Christopher's School in Bahrain with responsibility for wellbeing, behaviour and pastoral care. His recent Masters in Educational Leadership and Management Research examined why wellbeing programmes can often fail in schools – a topic he has presented and spoken on at conferences around the Middle East in the last two years.

Born in Nottingham, he spent the early part of his career acting in local films and theatre before working professionally as an actor in London. It was while working on a Theatre in Education production, delivering drama workshops in schools and youth centres in the East End of London, that he first developed a love for teaching. After re-training as an English teacher, Jamie specialised in the pastoral care of children and young people, working as a head of year in schools in Nottingham and Bahrain before becoming Assistant Head with oversight of whole-school wellbeing and pastoral systems.

FOREWORD

'You don't know what you've got 'til it's gone' has been the refrain of philosophers, poets, parents and politicians down through history. And with a person's mental and physical health this is especially true.

The best schools in any culture have always placed pastoral care and academic excellence side by side in their mission statements and daily practices. Arguably, the advent of the global pandemic – with children and young people studying in their homes not classrooms for far too long – threw a focus on wellbeing as never before.

Today, teachers and leaders around the globe are giving great thought to the subject of wellbeing, drawing on research and their own practices to ensure that no child comes to school and feels unsupported with their mental and physical health.

Those of us steeped in education – in special schools, primary schools, secondary schools and colleges – often say that students are the future, so obviously it matters how we take care of them on both a daily basis and through policies and practices across the system. Furthermore, as educationists we reflect that if we are truly exercised about our global future, we should be concerned about the present conditions of children across the world, not least those suffering as a result of poverty or conflict.

A word I hear often from UK and international school leaders is 'belonging'. They are reflecting on that word in animated discussions about student non-attendance. Leaders everywhere are wrestling with a post-Covid sentiment that while families and children still value education, everyday attendance in the place called school is not essential to making academic progress. Anecdotal and data evidence to that effect is ubiquitous.

And yet, 'belonging' lies deep in the human psyche. Leaders and teachers who recognise this provide irresistible learning environments so that students want to attend for fear of missing out on what their peers are enjoying. An integral part of irresistible classrooms is how schools innovatively and creatively work with children and young people to ensure they are in the best frame of mind for learning.

The A–Z of Student Wellbeing offers an authoritative and contemporary panorama of how the best schools, leaders and teachers work with their students and achieve great things, in essence securing *all* our futures. Happy students in any school are fun to be with, comfortable in their own skins, respectful of their peers and their teachers, and thrive socially and academically.

In common with all titles in the A–Z series, Section One is ordered around the 26 A–Z alphabetical headings. Section Two presents fascinating and practical materials for professional application in any setting.

As author Jamie O'Dowd takes us from **Atmosphere** to **Domino**, from **Illbeing** to **Jenga**, from **PERMA** to **Zzz**, his command of research, international current practice and, vitally, current knowledge of classrooms in action, radiates from every page. The 'Asides' that conclude each chapter are especially informative and fun.

The truism goes that no school system is better than its teachers. Equally true is that great relationships and positive wellbeing lie at the heart of vibrant and healthy classroom cultures, in any and every context where teachers and their students gather together.

Roy Blatchford, series editor

SECTION ONE

ATMOSPHERE

When you first set your heart on becoming a teacher, you might have imagined your classroom as a picture-book, idyllic sanctuary, full of happy, eager-to-learn children who adored being in your company. Growing up, I assumed that every teacher set out to be like Miss Honey (from Roald Dahl's *Matilda*) but somehow ended up embittered and twisted by the job, becoming more like Miss Trunchbull as each year passed. Thirty years later, I still feel I was partially right.

Critics of wellbeing could argue that it is too abstract and complex a concept to be simplified in an A–Z format like this. So, what better way to begin than with something that is indeed abstract but also fundamental and complex all at once: the atmosphere in a classroom.

As teachers, we are in the privileged position of being the rulers of our own domains. Our classrooms are our workspaces for most of the day. Aside from a rushed coffee break in the morning and, more often than not, a working lunch, we create a home for ourselves and our students in these spaces. The atmosphere in these hallowed rooms directly influences how safe and secure a pupil feels, which, in turn, affects their wellbeing. Establishing this core element of emotional security helps create an atmosphere conducive to both learning and emotional development.

It is possible to walk down a school corridor, visit 10 different classrooms and experience 10 distinct atmospheres in as many minutes, such is the richness and complexity of a school's ecosystem. This variety is part of what makes the school experience so special and should be celebrated – but only when these atmospheres are consistently positive and conducive to wellbeing. Students have an uncanny ability to assess the atmosphere of a classroom in the time it takes to enter, sit down and take out their pencil cases or laptops. They will adjust their behaviour and expectations quickly based on their initial impressions.

FIRST IMPRESSIONS

The first three minutes can set the tone for the rest of the lesson. A pupil's natural ability to assess the atmosphere becomes heightened during this time, and they will subconsciously draw all sorts of inferences from factors such as:

- the teacher's mood, body language, facial expressions and tone of voice
- how, when and where they are greeted
- the layout of the classroom
- classroom displays
- the type of starter activity being used
- how the register is taken
- what is displayed on the board
- how the learning from the previous lesson is recalled or recapped
- how the main task is introduced
- how questions are used.

Apart from the first few days of the school year, students will likely arrive with preconceived expectations of the atmosphere in your classroom, based on their relationship with you and your standing in the school. If you are unsure how your pupils perceive the atmosphere, a simple student voice activity can help. Using a Likert scale, you could ask them to respond to statements like:

'I look forward to coming to this class/lesson.'

'Mr/Mrs/Miss/Ms cares as much about me as they do about my progress/learning.'

'Mr/Mrs/Miss/Ms tries to make lessons enjoyable for us.'

'I feel safe when I'm in this classroom.'

'I can tell that Mr/Mrs/Miss/Ms enjoys teaching us.'

ATMOSPHERE

A useful task when visiting a new school is to ask the students to name a teacher whose class they enjoy the most. In just five minutes, it is likely you will see more effective wellbeing practices in that classroom than during the rest of your visit. The simple techniques below can contribute to creating an outstanding classroom atmosphere and are easy to observe when visiting different schools and classrooms.

You might want to consider the following list of small changes that could positively impact the atmosphere in your classroom:

- Students are greeted at the door.
- The teacher knows something about most students and asks personalised questions as they enter: 'How did tennis go last night?'; 'Are you feeling better?'; 'How are you feeling about your team losing again at the weekend?'
- Upbeat music is playing quietly as students enter.
- Instead of a traditional register, students move name cards to a column with different 'emoji' moods as headers. The teacher completes the register once the students are working, using this as a quick mood snapshot.
- The interactive whiteboard displays a positive message, such as 'Welcome to Monday Maths!', with a brainteaser to engage students as they enter.
- The starter activity reviews previous work and is a fun, team-based online quiz (e.g., Kahoot! or Blooket).
- The teacher rarely stays behind their desk, preferring to move among the students, participating in the action.
- Low-level disruption is addressed discreetly while the rest of the class continues working, with clear instructions given.
- The teacher speaks excitedly about the task and the challenges ahead.
- Humour is used appropriately, with students responding warmly.
- There is a clear sense of teamwork between teacher and pupils.
- Students speak more than the teacher, and they are encouraged to challenge or be challenged by each other's contributions.

- Motivation is maintained by the promise of a reward at the end of the lesson, often another subject-related game.

The atmosphere in a class like this is already structured and organised in a way that promotes wellbeing right from the point of entry – yet everything in this list is simple and tangible. When the teacher of such a class increases the difficulty of learning later in the lesson, an atmosphere has already been established where students feel safe to take risks because the teacher has them engaged and onboard. Students in these types of classrooms will tell you they feel important, safe and cared for by the teacher. Imagine a real-life 'Miss Honey', but without the over-the-top fairy-tale sweetness of Roald Dahl's story.

WHO CONTROLS THE CLIMATE?

Now, think about your own experiences in the world of work. Who do you enjoy collaborating with and why? Who motivates you and gets the best out of you? Which workplaces have you enjoyed working at, and where have the hours dragged?

All of these people and places created their own atmosphere, resulting in your positive or negative responses. A student's school experience is very similar. As teachers, we must acknowledge that we control the weather in our classrooms, not the students. We are the sunshine, the rain clouds, the thunder or the lightning, depending on the relationships, language and habits that have become 'norms' with our group of students.

During Covid, one of the things many students said they missed most about school was the 'normal' interactions with their teachers. As learning moved online and teachers became cautious about who might be listening, relationships often suffered. Teacher–pupil banter diminished as many colleagues feared something being taken out of context on camera by adults listening in. This reminds us that relationships rely on seemingly insignificant conversations, and that these are key to the classroom atmosphere.

We shouldn't underestimate the importance of small talk – the conversations about the weekend, last night's TV or the weather. These are the building blocks of relationships and atmosphere, but they can be lost under the increasing pressure to deliver curriculum content and meet targets.

A positive atmosphere cannot be created without authenticity. In many ways, it's the end result of putting all the other elements of this book into practice. Young people won't be fooled into believing an adult cares if they truly don't. There's no 'tick-box' list for creating a positive atmosphere; students can see through insincerity instantly. Your classroom's atmosphere is a reflection of you as a teacher, and it needs to be cared for and nurtured, just like the students in it.

ASIDE

It's easy to blush and graciously accept a parent's praise at a parents' evening, 'Jenny loves your class!', before quickly moving on. But take the time to understand the origins of these sentiments. If you can, ask 'Why?'. You may learn more about your classroom atmosphere than you expect. Most comments won't be about your teaching, your wonderful displays or the laminated flashcards you send home every week; they will usually reflect how you make their child feel, which is indirect feedback about your classroom's atmosphere.

Should you ever find yourself on the receiving end of less-favourable feedback, try not to be disheartened. Politely ask the same question: 'Could you tell me why they feel that way about being in my class?'. You'll learn more from this than you might imagine, even if it's tough to hear. It happens to the best of us at some point in our careers!

BEHAVIOUR

This chapter is brought to you by the three Cs: consistency, clarity and calmness, the cornerstones of any well-managed classroom.

Pupils' behaviour is often cited as one of the main reasons why adults are reluctant to pursue or remain in a career in education, and it is a key factor driving teachers to leave the profession. For those who struggle with behaviour management, the skills required to maintain order in the classroom can seem abstract and intangible. For those who manage behaviour effectively, it can feel instinctive, and when asked, 'What's your secret?', they may stare blankly and offer a humble, often dismissive, excuse.

Those who struggle with behaviour often shift the blame onto the 'naughty kids', 'awful parents' or 'school leaders who give no support'. Yet, if you gather together all the adults who work with a certain poorly behaved pupil and ask about their behaviour, you'll likely find that one or two teachers report the same pupil's behaviour as absolutely fine. So, how is this possible? How can a child behave so badly in one class and be angelic in another, within the space of a morning or afternoon?

The aim here is not to take you through a crash course in behaviour management, but to explore the link between behaviour and a student whose wellbeing needs are not being met. Great wellbeing practice in the classroom recognises the role of *all* behaviour, not just *good* behaviour – although, of course, good behaviour makes everything easier for the teacher and the other students. The behaviour of pupils in your class can offer insight into their wellbeing and provide clues about their mental health needs. Depending on your viewpoint, the old adage 'There's no such thing as a naughty child' could be a useful starting point.

Maslow's hierarchy of needs

Think of a student you've worked with whose needs, according to Maslow's hierarchy, were not being met. Or, let's bring it closer to home: think of a time when your safety or physiological needs, or those of your family, were threatened. What instincts kicked in? How did your behaviour differ in those situations compared to your usual behaviour in the classroom or in professional settings? It would be fair to assume the change was significant. Even the meekest adults can turn to aggression when those closest to them are in danger. Mothers of very young children often provide the most extreme examples of this as their instincts to defend and protect can bring out the animal within them.

As humans, our behaviour is shaped by our needs and influenced by our mental health and wellbeing at any given time. Behaviour is often a symptom of a deeper issue. Students experiencing mental health issues or other wellbeing challenges may feel threatened, particularly in relation to their needs at the bottom of Maslow's hierarchy. In fact, fear or perceived threats are often the root cause of many of the behaviours teachers consider undesirable. These behaviours may signal that a student's needs are not being met, either inside or outside of school. Rather than rushing to punish, it might be more helpful to explore the underlying causes, as summarised in Table 1.

Table 1 The relationship between student behaviour and unsatisfied needs

Student behaviour	Threat of fear they may be experiencing	Which need is not being met
Physical/violent	Threat to their own safety Fear of being hurt	The need to be safe; the need to be loved
Cheating/lying	Threat to their own safety Fear of not being good enough	The need to be understood; the need to be themselves
Stealing	Threat to their physiological needs Fear of 'not having' sufficient resources	The need to have suitable resources
Poor attitude to teachers	Threat to their sense of love and belonging Fear of not being respected	The need to connect with others
Poor attitude to peers	Threat to their self-esteem Fear of not being accepted/a defence mechanism	The need to develop relationships
Lack of engagement	Threat to their self-actualisation Fear of failure	The need to be recognised/rewarded

Let's now return to the three Cs and consider how adult behaviours can positively impact a pupil's wellbeing, even during challenging moments.

CONSISTENCY

A pupil's wellbeing is promoted when behaviour management is consistent in the classroom. Uncertainty about what mood a teacher will be in or what kind of classroom environment they will enter can cause anxiety. As creatures of habit, children benefit from consistency, which helps embed positive behaviours. Without consistency, engagement becomes difficult as pupils remain on high alert, trying to decode the environment and potential threats.

For example, last week when Lisa wrote 'Fart' on the whiteboard, Miss X found it endearingly cheeky and mildly admonished her with a grin. Today, when Alex did the same thing, Miss X was furious. Alex was sent out of class, his parents were called in and he faced consequences. The students, now on edge, are unsure where the boundaries lie with a teacher they once felt safe with. This inconsistency threatens their sense of safety and may become a barrier to learning.

CLARITY

When students are unable to understand those around them or have difficulty communicating, frustration can often lead to inappropriate behaviour. Clarity is important for several reasons:

- **Comprehension:** Children are still developing their language and comprehension skills all the way through their school journey and into adulthood, so it is important to use clear, simple language. Ambiguity can lead to confusion and anxiety.
- **Learning:** Clear communication models support effective language, learning and behaviour. This is especially important for neurodiverse students and students for whom English is a second language. For all students, language is the gateway to learning and the teacher who is unable to explain and issue instructions necessary for teaching and learning will undoubtedly encounter problems.
- **Engagement and participation:** When communication is clear, students tend to be more engaged and involved. Clear and positive communication enables a student to access the learning effectively and encourages engagement and participation. In the absence of clarity, students are likely to disengage and their self-esteem can suffer if they feel they are unable to process and follow instructions.
- **Emotional connection:** Children depend on very clear and direct communication in order to understand emotions and social cues. Expressing yourself clearly allows students to pick up on the emotional tone of your message, which helps promote a deeper emotional connection and understanding. Instructions/expectations that are clear and concise, when used in favour of emotional rants, show you are in control of the situation and help a child feel safe.
- **Trust:** Language use that is consistent and clear helps build trust between the pupil and the teacher. This is necessary for a positive classroom environment. Flashes of sarcasm or language that demeans or patronises forces the pupil into a shell to protect

themself from possible embarrassment or emotional distress. Even when used jokingly, this can affect a pupil's ability to extend trust in that relationship.
- **Developmental stage:** Adapting language to the student's developmental stage avoids confusion and promotes understanding. Children develop at different rates and this is why differentiation has been a key focus for most schools over the last few years. We are seeing students make better progress in their learning when the language used to instruct matches their developmental age and not just their chronological age.
- **Self-expression:** Clear communication encourages children to express themselves confidently. Having an adult model this constantly provides them with an example that they can follow and, as a result, they will mirror how they are spoken to in their responses to their peers and their teacher.

CALMNESS

It cannot be overstated how important it is to a pupil's wellbeing to have an adult calmly lead them through whatever storm it is they need shelter from at that time.

Whatever the incident is that has resulted in a pupil becoming distressed, everything must be shelved in favour of returning the distressed pupil to a calm state in the midst of an incident. Sorting out the fight and who-hit-who first can wait. It doesn't matter for now who stole Rebecca's lunch box and put it in the rabbit hutch – the priority is restoring a sense of calm and order. Nothing was ever resolved through floods of tears, the fear of sanctions or the worry of adults being 'cross' about what had just happened. Emotions run high, poor decisions are made and recollections of instigating contexts are clouded through the upset and anguish in the immediate aftermath of an incident taking place.

Effective wellbeing cannot be practised in the eye of the storm. Nothing needs to happen until a sense of calm is restored. Little can be achieved through the snot, the tears and the sobs, as much as it is our instinct to try to drag the child quickly out of their anguish and fix the problem for them.

'I can see that you are upset, I am just going to give you some time to breathe and calm yourself down, only then will we talk about this further. There's no rush. Take your time.'

To the pupil, this puts the emphasis on their wellbeing over the resolution of the issue. In the time it takes a pupil to calm down, reflection has already begun and the process that follows is more efficient and reliable as a result. Compare this to the teacher who leads with, 'Stop crying now! Max is in the nurse's room with a black eye, his parents are on the way so I need to get to the bottom of this immediately.' When cornered, the threat level increases, the resultant behaviour will be unpredictable and the pupil will be responding under duress.

Calm communication reduces stress for both the pupil and the adult. When adults speak in a calm tone, it helps to de-escalate tense situations and creates a more positive atmosphere. This can prevent unnecessary stress and anxiety for the pupil. When teachers do this, we are modelling effective communication with the hope that this is then emulated by the pupil in their own interactions. We are also modelling regulation and giving security around how issues are dealt with.

A classroom that operates positively in these three areas is still not necessarily a classroom devoid of behaviour-management challenges. There is no magic wand when it comes to behaviour and the aim of the teacher or of a school should not be to eradicate *all* poor behaviour from the school; 'some' is entirely normal, even 'healthy' to a certain extent.

We are, after all, dealing with human beings not robots. Learning and development takes place as part of the handling and resolution of a behavioural issue and, when done correctly, this can have a positive impact on a pupil's wellbeing in the longer term as boundaries are discovered and models of how to deal with conflict are presented and reinforced.

ASIDE

Behaviour for learning

Reflection after an incident is crucial. Whether your school adopts a restorative approach or not, little will be learned by the pupil by simply losing a playtime, logging the misdemeanour on your school's system or emailing home. Reflection is critical:

1. What led to you doing what you did?
2. How did you feel at the time?
3. How do you feel now?
4. Why does this matter?
5. Who has been hurt as a result of your behaviour?
6. How can we fix this now it is over?
7. What skills do we need to work on to make sure this is handled better next time?

Connecting the incident, their emotions and how this might change (improve) future occurrences promotes wellbeing by showing the pupil that there can be a positive outcome to what may have been a distressing or out-of-character behaviour.

CHARACTER

WHAT ARE CHARACTER STRENGTHS?

A useful exercise in any school is to take a sample of reports from each year group and examine the balance between positive comments and targets for improvement. Typically, in schools, in the early years, the positives outweigh the targets by a ratio of around 10:1. As this same pupil progresses through infant and junior school, this ratio tends to balance out. By the time the student reaches senior school, the reports often show a shift, with the ratio favouring targets and areas for improvement over positive comments about their character and personality.

Ironically, at a time in their development when teenagers desperately need positive reinforcement about themselves more than ever, the focus shifts increasingly towards how they should improve their learning and grades, with fewer comments celebrating their development into adolescence.

Character strengths are fundamental components of the human experience, studied extensively in psychology, philosophy and education. Understanding character strengths is beneficial for personal development, positive psychology and fostering a healthy society, particularly when we tune into recognising and rewarding the good in others. As educators, we are skilled at identifying these traits in the pupils we know well, and we often use them informally in daily interactions: the 'kind' pupil is chosen to be the 'buddy' for the new starter, the 'natural leader' often ends up on the student council, and those with a 'love of learning' frequently find themselves speaking to visiting inspectors and VIPs!

Each of us has a 'signature' set of character strengths, of which there are 24, grouped into six core virtues as shown in the figure. You and your students can discover your signature strengths by taking a quick (and free) survey at www.viacharacter.org. Students love finding out their strengths, and it's a fun and engaging exercise to see if they can predict their own strengths (and those of their friends and teachers) before taking the survey.

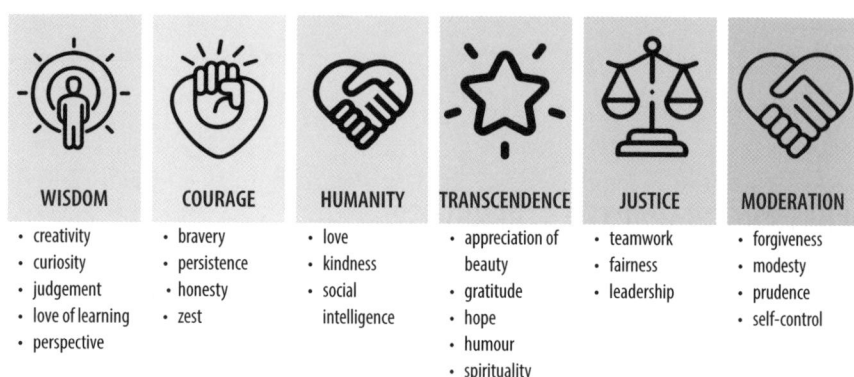

WISDOM	COURAGE	HUMANITY	TRANSCENDENCE	JUSTICE	MODERATION
• creativity • curiosity • judgement • love of learning • perspective	• bravery • persistence • honesty • zest	• love • kindness • social intelligence	• appreciation of beauty • gratitude • hope • humour • spirituality	• teamwork • fairness • leadership	• forgiveness • modesty • prudence • self-control

Character strengths
Adapted from Al Taher, 2016, Character Strengths and Virtues: The Classification Explained

CHARACTER STRENGTHS AND WELLBEING

When a student knows their character strengths, there is an immediate positive impact on their wellbeing from having these strengths recognised, celebrated and spoken about. One school successfully incorporated this by giving each student a sticker for their three signature strengths, which were proudly displayed on the front of their books or laptops for all to see. At a glance, the class teacher could then employ these strengths in discussions, when distributing team roles or when allocating classroom jobs. Making it visual kept it at the forefront of discussion.

Each week the school focused on a different character strength to encourage deeper discussion and understanding of the true meaning of the trait. Famous people, past and present, who utilised these strengths in their success were highlighted to exemplify and celebrate these traits in action. This shared vocabulary helped foster resilience and understanding. In a short time, students were using this language to make sense of their own actions and behaviours, as well as those of others around them.

CHARACTER STRENGTHS IN ACTION

Character strengths are positive traits or attributes that contribute to an individual's moral, intellectual and social wellbeing. These strengths are considered morally valuable and contribute to a person's overall positive functioning. They are the building blocks of a person's character and play a significant role in shaping an individual's thoughts, feelings and behaviours.

One of the most influential classification systems is the VIA Classification of Strengths, developed by Peterson and Seligman (2004). This classification identifies 24 character strengths organised under six broad virtues:

- Wisdom
- Humanity
- Transcendence
- Justice
- Moderation.

Each virtue includes several specific character strengths, such as creativity, bravery, kindness, fairness, self-regulation and spirituality. Focusing on these strengths promotes wellbeing by helping a pupil understand themselves and highlighting the traits that make them unique. In some schools, students take this survey twice a year, and it is fascinating to see how their personal development influences the ranking of their 24 strengths as they grow into young adults.

However, there is a danger of treating character strengths as a passing trend. Some teachers may dismiss the concept as such. Yet, in reality, we celebrate character strengths daily, often without the need for a formal label or in-depth knowledge of the underlying theory proposed by Peterson and Seligman. The categories are useful tools to explore with your students, raising self-awareness and the ability to recognise strengths in others.

In the United Arab Emirates (UAE), for example, they have adopted the notion of character strengths nationwide to align with their national vision of creating a knowledge-based, inclusive and happy society. The US Army also employs a more-advanced version of the character strengths assessment, called the Global Assessment Tool (GAT), which assesses soldiers' strengths in various domains, including emotional, social, spiritual and family fitness. The GAT helps soldiers identify strengths like courage, perseverance and self-regulation, providing personalised training to enhance these strengths. If entire nations and military organisations are using such assessments to better understand and develop their people, there is a strong argument for schools to adopt similar practices to better understand and nurture our students.

ASIDE

Character strengths are to be celebrated. The survey will rank a person's character strengths from 1st to 24th. Schools would be advised to focus on the strengths and not make it a requirement that students work to develop those character strengths that are in their bottom three. This is not the purpose of this particular concept. It turns something that is designed to be positive into yet another target that must be attained for the school to feel a sense of having developed or accomplished something for their students.

Having character strengths in the lower half of their ranking does not mean these students aren't 'good' or 'strong' in those areas, it just means other strengths are more meaningful and prominent in terms of who they are. Take humour, for example. We simply can't all be funny — I've been trying for years and have got absolutely nowhere in developing that trait, or so my students, family and colleagues regularly tell me.

1. **Identify and highlight strengths frequently:** Start by helping students to recognise their own character strengths, such as patience, kindness or curiosity. Use activities such as strength-awareness exercises, where students are encouraged to identify strengths employed by others in stories or real life. Encourage them to notice and appreciate the strengths in their friends as well.

2. **Incorporate strengths into lessons:** Embed character strengths into your curriculum by tying them to classroom topics and activities. For example, discuss how they help the characters in stories or history lessons reach their goals. How can character strengths be employed in solving mathematical problems or improving teamwork and collaboration on group projects?
3. **Use strengths in feedback:** Provide feedback that acknowledges and reinforces the student's use of character strengths. Instead of focusing on academic performance alone, reward qualities such as honesty, flexibility, endurance or enthusiasm. Phrases like 'I appreciate your patience in solving that difficult problem' help students understand the value of their strengths and focus on the process, not just the result.
4. **Model strengths as a teacher:** Demonstrate character strengths in your actions. Show empathy in difficult conversations or be creative in planning lessons; make those strengths explicit when you talk about them. Share experiences of how using your strengths helped you overcome challenges or improve yourself.
5. **Create opportunities to develop strengths:** Create classroom activities and challenges that give students opportunities to use and develop their strengths and make these explicit. Group students according to their strengths and refer to them in the learning objectives. Promote collaborative problem-solving by providing leadership roles and planning projects that require specific strengths to be employed. Give students roles based on their strengths so they feel good about having to put them to positive use.

DOMINO

'Television blamed for suicide rise'

Headline from *The Guardian*, Sunday 18 April, 2004

I once attended a mental health conference in the UK that left me feeling quite uncomfortable. At that time, more than 20 years ago, a speaker attributed the rise in the number of students self-harming to what he had coined the 'Hollyoaks effect'.

For those unfamiliar with this cultural phenomenon, *Hollyoaks* is a TV soap opera that is aimed at the teen/young adult market. In its heyday, it was very popular and gained a sizeable following, especially among younger viewers. This programme often found itself tackling controversial and taboo topics such as abuse, drug use, sexual assault and incest. Over the years, many storylines have featured characters who self-harmed or were suicidal.

It was with some surprise that I heard a mental health expert correlate the rise in numbers of teenagers self-harming to this television programme's storylines and growing popularity, with very little in the way of evidence.

In 2008, the 'Bridgend Suicides' made national and global headlines following 20 suicides of young people aged between 15 and 29 in the first six months of the year (Luce, 2016). So how did the authorities account for this sharp upturn in young people taking their own lives? The lazy response was to blame it on storylines in programmes such as *Hollyoaks*. The parents of one of those who took their own life went as far as accusing the media of 'glamourising ways of taking one's life to young people' – hence the use of the term 'the Hollyoaks effect' by this particular mental health expert all those years ago.

During adolescence, young people are typically more influenced by their peers than by any other social group, including their parents. This chapter does not claim that teens will blindly copy one another in such damaging behaviours as self-harm (some believed this to be true many years ago, but we now accept this as a myth), but it may trigger something in those with underlying mental health issues or unresolved trauma.

If a friend shares positive experiences or feelings of relief/satisfaction after any type of damaging behaviour (getting drunk or self-harming, for example) it carries the potential to seem appealing to those yet to have experienced or experimented with this behaviour, particularly in young people who are already vulnerable or experiencing their own challenges mentally.

It is reductive to blame the decline in young people's mental health solely at the door of the media. However, it is essential that we do not underestimate the impact of external influences on how children and young people frame their own wellbeing and mental health. Social media has since replaced television as the 'folk devil' when it comes to negative influences bombarding the youth of today with problematic and dangerous messages that have the potential to affect their wellbeing and mental health.

It is indisputable that schools have a role to play in educating young people about the power of social media. The pressure is also now on the social media giants to regulate and adjust algorithms so that those seeking out any positive reinforcement about dangerous behaviours around self-harm, eating disorders or sexualised behaviour are not bombarded with inappropriate content. Sadly, it would appear we are still some way off any sort of responsible and effective regulation. Increasingly, we are seeing schools banning the use of mobile phones on site, though the issue of how children are impacted by images and videos that affect their sense of self remains something that is not fully understood, even by experts.

On the flip side, while not as powerful as social media, schools still have the ability to develop positive wellbeing habits that can create a domino effect in a healthier direction.

When I was a new teacher, many years ago, one of my first classes guffawed, sniggered and eye-rolled their way through a starter activity

I attempted, with the aim of introducing some very basic breathing techniques. It was a similar embarrassed response when I attempted 'two-minute table-time yoga' the week after. The gratitude plenary wasn't taken seriously either so, in my fragile inexperience and feeling defeated, I gave in. Until a colleague in the staffroom told me that the same students who had been dismissive of the activities were asking for it in other classes. I realised then that I had simply not persevered or allowed enough time for this to become embedded. Eventually, I was asked to share these techniques at the next whole-staff meeting so others could try them and it resulted in further mindfulness and wellbeing activities being used as starters and plenaries more frequently in the school.

Where many schools fail when attempting to change their culture to one that promotes and celebrates wellbeing, is by trying to do too much, too quickly. Culture change, by its very nature, is complex and time consuming, and students can find it disorienting if too many changes are attempted at the same time. Students (and staff) need to be guided through a whole-school change in a way that gradually incorporates wellbeing activities one-by-one rather than having many activities forced upon them all at once.

If the fundamentals of a school's culture are not in place prior to the implementation of a wellbeing programme, individual teacher efforts will be in vain. These fundamentals include positive staff wellbeing, positive and trusting relationships between staff and students, and a genuine collective belief in wellbeing from the governors through to the dinner ladies, admin staff and cleaners. Schools attempting to implement more-advanced wellbeing concepts before securing this wellbeing 'base' will find that their attempts will falter.

Where wellbeing is implemented successfully, the domino effect can be successful in enabling positivity around a particular intervention or activity to spread, before the next intervention or activity is introduced. Particularly in the post-Covid era, schools were in such a rush to 'do wellbeing well' that it had the counter effect and programmes, events and activities were often poorly thought out and ineffective.

To echo Simon Sinek (2011), for such a domino effect to be positive, the first question a school should be asking itself is 'why'. Why are we collapsing the timetable today to hold a wellbeing day? Why is the wellbeing speaker coming in today with no preparation, follow-up or evaluation? Why are we marking World Mental Health Day? Are we just ticking the boxes in our school development plan for the year where we set ourselves the target of promoting wellbeing more effectively with one-off initiatives? If so, your one-day collapsed timetable or guest speaker will have very little effect. In fact, the domino effect will not be activated and the impact will be negligible.

> **ASIDE**
>
> Research tells us that children do not self-harm or commit suicide because they have seen it on TV, in a film or because their friends have spoken about it. Positive reinforcement around dangerous behaviours, especially online, is a growing concern, however. Schools can be proactive by taking decisive steps to implement wellbeing practices, policies and programmes that are sustainable.
>
> 1. Plan wellbeing programmes that follow the distributed learning model. Talk about wellbeing on the first day of school and share the plan and strategy for the year ahead with students and parents in the first week of the year. Start by ensuring every member of the school community understands the basic grammar about wellbeing, even if it means starting with the very word itself! You'll be amazed by how many people misunderstand it.
> 2. Expert speakers, expensive wellbeing software/platforms, wellbeing committees and wellbeing awards/accreditations should not be considered until the community first fully understands the school's holistic approach to wellbeing.
> 3. Getting parents on board is essential in creating a domino effect. When parents understand and can discuss the wellbeing concepts that are taught in school at home, everything starts moving in the right direction. Getting parents on board is essential and they must be considered early in your plan.

4. Keep reinforcing key messages at carefully timed intervals throughout the year. Wellbeing should not just be the domain of the class teacher, form tutor, the head of year or for circle time. There is no reason why wellbeing cannot run as a theme through maths, English, science, history, geography, art, drama, music and PE.

5. Modelling as an adult is essential in normalising wellbeing practices, language and behaviour. Don't give in if your box-breathing starter is initially met with laughter. Persevere and explain the science, the methodology and the research at a level your class can understand. Add a contemporary perspective to your activity by using YouTube to find clips of positive/famous role models talking about their experiences of the benefit of wellbeing and mindfulness techniques.

ENGAGEMENT

Among the many complex strands that combine to help a child grow and develop, engagement is a pivotal thread that brings together cognitive, emotional, social and physical development. Engagement is essential for a child's wellbeing as it plays a fundamental role in their overall growth and happiness. As teachers, we already understand engagement to be a primary ingredient in the learning process and we know that students who are engaged can find meaning and purpose in their learning and achieve improved outcomes and progress as a result.

If our students are engaged, it means they are engrossed in activities, thinking, learning or socialising in a way that interests them and captures their imagination. Throughout childhood, engagement aids growth and sets the stage for a journey that encompasses not just academic achievements but also the holistic development of character, resilience and happiness. Childhood should be full of awe and wonder; being engaged is something that occurs naturally, initially, and becomes more difficult to achieve as we grow and become desensitised to the stimuli around us.

To nurture a pupil's ability to engage, a teacher must first know what it is that engages them. That is not to say we should pander only to an individual's preferences and tastes, but knowing what makes a child (or children in general) 'tick' certainly takes some of the mystery and guesswork away. Through character strengths, there are opportunities to engage students through utilising one of their 'signature strengths', and when this is made explicit by the teacher, increased levels of motivation are often the reward. Children thrive when using a strength, be it a skill, talent or a character trait.

'Do not train a child to learn by force or harshness; but direct them to it by what amuses their minds.'

Attributed to Plato

There is a sweet spot that exists – a place where student engagement is magically activated – when all the other stars in the educational universe align. This is a time when students (and the teacher) enter a state of flow, where time passes so quickly and no one wants to hear the bell for the end of the lesson, such is the focus and engagement on the task. When a teacher 'strikes gold' in this way, it could be easy to dismiss it as 'just a really good lesson' or that students and teacher 'were on form' that day.

Such magical moments cannot be left to chance as we chase this 'sweet spot' every day of our teaching lives. There is some science to it to help demystify these magical moments and by better understanding the contributory factors, we are able to achieve engagement in our students more frequently.

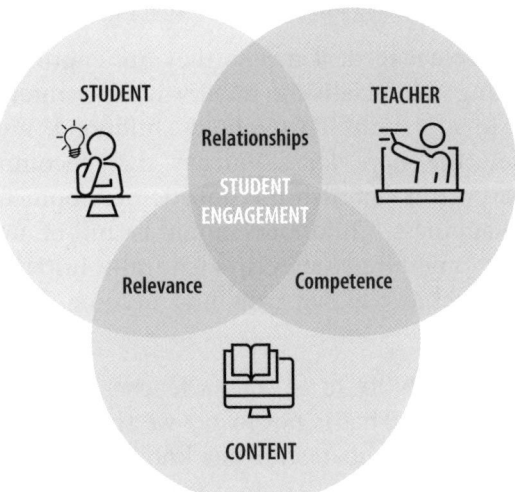

Student engagement

There must first of all be a relationship between the teacher and the student whereby trust exists, as well as the teacher having a sense of belief in the child's capabilities. The student must find the content relevant and challenging – there must be an intrinsic reason for them to want to *know* the information or develop the skill. Finally, of no small consequence, the teacher must be competent in their knowledge of the content, their ability to pitch the relevance of it to the student, and they must design activities that lead the student through the various stages of the learning.

And, if you are lucky enough to have all of this fall into place, you simply need to hope and pray that all the other variables outside of your control don't hijack your lesson: no fight at breaktime that is the talk of the class, no sudden snow storm, no dog in the playground or any of the other amazing little distractions that can throw a class into disarray!

We are, first and foremost, places of education and, despite all of the currency that wellbeing has gained in the post-Covid era, learning will continue to be our core business. Yet there is a natural synergy that exists between the two; so powerful to learning is wellbeing and vice versa. Think back to when you or your own child learned to ride a bike for the first time, swam those first nervous metres without armbands or took those first wobbly steps. The acquisition or mastery of a skill is incredibly powerful and the impact on our sense of self, our confidence and self-esteem is as effective as any wellbeing intervention that exists. In an ideal world, a child's wellbeing needs could be met through positive relationships, play and learning alone. If only it was as simple as that!

We are, of course, living in a world where the technology surrounding our children often feels like too much of a formidable competitor. Social media is designed in such a way that instant gratification is expected by the user, and the algorithms are ruthless in their ability to constantly serve up content that can engage the user. There is overwhelming evidence that this has a negative impact on a child's attention span and ability to focus and engage when detached from their digital devices.

Schools are now increasingly concerned about the impact of phone addiction, with many countries in Europe already moving to ban phones in schools and the UK now looking set to follow suit. It is easy to fall in line with an alarmist response to this technological threat but it does not change the fact that young people have *always* wanted to be effectively engaged in learning and play. No child comes to school hoping to spend the day completely bored and disengaged.

The modern teacher has to be more creative than ever before in finding ways to engage today's children. If you were raised in a time before the internet, you will recall that all that needed to happen in your own junior school classroom to engage the class was for the TV and video cabinet to be rolled out. When that happened, the class knew they were in for a treat because they were going to get to watch something on the screen! We now appreciate that many children can only focus on one task for anything as low as 10 minutes (6–7 years old); this rises to around 30 minutes for teenagers.

So, to really engage students, lessons need to change pace and be varied in the type of activity students are being asked to complete. The learning also needs to be about something they feel is worth investing in. What will they get out of this in the end? Will this be a skill or knowledge that they really want to acquire? If not, why would they bother?

Great wellbeing practice in the classroom is somewhat reliant on students being engaged. A student's concern about threats and unmet needs, which can result in behaviour problems, can be suspended temporarily when a student is engaged in learning, especially if they enter a state of flow where all that matters is the task or activity that has inspired them. History is littered with famous people who used their skill or passion as a means to cope with trauma or a mental health issue because it was their escape route from the pain they endured. The children suffering in your classrooms are no different.

Sadly, and here I risk jumping on the 'anti-technology bandwagon' again, young people have forgotten how to self-regulate and utilise their passions as a means of addressing fears, concerns or anxieties. We do see students entering a state of flow when gaming or when engrossed in catching up on social media. In the past, reading, outdoor pursuits, crafts, sports, music and other hobbies were what naturally engaged young people. These are rapidly being replaced by technology. We can, in the classroom, re-engage students in finding awe and wonder in the world around them, and reconnect them with one another and the environment by creating activities that are meaningful and impactful.

ASIDE

Case study

The Year 13 Media Studies class were having an enlightening conversation with their teacher about what they missed most about being children and, in particular, what they missed about being a younger student in the school. One thing they all agreed on was that they missed being read to. Whether by a parent or by a teacher, they missed the act of experiencing a story as a collective; they missed the ability to share emotions at the same time as their peers in the class – the gasps of surprise, the laughter in response to a joke, the shared heartbreak or joy of the resolution.

In agreement with the class teacher, they made it a point from that day forward that they would always end the lesson with one of them sharing something they had read recently with the rest of the group. It varied from news reports to short stories to articles about the media industry. It was a return to a basic activity that they had previously felt that they had outgrown. Ultimately, this wasn't really about the reading at all – it was about engagement, relationships and the coming together of a class to share and experience emotions. The teacher could never have imagined ending a lesson with a bunch of 17/18-year-old students with 'story time', but the impact on their engagement and wellbeing was significant.

1. Creating tasks that are engaging doesn't always require hours of complex preparation. Sometimes the element of surprise is what engages students. For example, how would your students react if the following was written on the board as they entered the classroom: 'You have 30 minutes to divide into two groups and prepare for a court case where we are putting the use of mobile phones on trial. Decide who is defending and who is prosecuting – I cannot speak until the timer reaches zero. Good luck.'

2. Sometimes, all it takes to engage the student is to fine-tune the task to make it appeal to their interests or hobbies. 'You have a budget of £1000. Can you successfully use this money to get to next weekend's F1 race in Italy? You must cover transport, ticket, accommodation and food costs.' An activity like this offers a real-world approach to using maths and budgeting in a way designed to appeal to the F1 fans in the class.
3. Student take overs are another great way to get small groups engaged by empowering them with a project to teach the rest of the class on a particular aspect of the topic you are studying. Putting them in the role of the teacher can change the dynamic of their engagement completely.

FLOURISHING

WHAT IS FLOURISHING?

The concept of flourishing goes beyond the mere absence of problems or distress and reaches deep into the positive end of the wellbeing spectrum. It encompasses the full scope of wellbeing, where individuals experience positive emotions, engage in meaningful activities, establish and maintain rewarding relationships, and achieve a sense of purpose and accomplishment in much of what they do. In the context of schools, flourishing translates into creating an environment where students not only succeed academically but also thrive personally, socially and emotionally.

Defining 'flourishing' can be as simple or as complex as you like. Perhaps the most accessible definition tells us that 'Flourishing is feeling good and doing good' (Seligman, 2012). Martin Seligman is the most significant figure in positive psychology, having coined the phrase himself in the 1990s.

He was baffled by the fact that we knew so much about what contributed to poor mental health and wellbeing, yet very few people had studied or conducted research into those fortunate enough to be at the positive end of the mental health continuum. What followed was decades of research into the conditions that enabled people to experience 'Authentic Happiness' (Seligman, 2002) and was eventually refined into the concept that we now call 'Flourishing'.

STRATEGIES FOR A FLOURISHING SCHOOL

Children need to understand the science around wellbeing from an early age. Making explicit links between their actions, their interactions and their achievements, to the positive feelings they produce, is essential in empowering young people to be proactive in maintaining healthy wellbeing practices for themselves as they become more independent. When we help young people to make conscious decisions about the actions they take to promote their happiness, we are contributing to the building of a generation whose self-efficacy is more powerful than any therapy or medication. Using the three concepts of 'actions', 'interactions' and 'achievements' as a starting point, schools can create the conditions needed to enable their young people to flourish.

Actions

Schools should reward and recognise positive actions that students engage in, beyond the academic. The school's policy on rewards should clearly set out a tiered system of rewards that recognise positive actions, including those that occur on a daily basis (and are, perhaps, often taken for granted), such as good manners, being kind and showing respect, to those that are more exceptional: raising money for charity, going above and beyond to help a friend, or representing the school.

Too often, schools expect these actions to be performed as a matter of course, almost as if they are default settings in our students, ignoring the fact that these values may not be instilled by some parents. Nevertheless, to build a flourishing school, these positive actions still need recognition to provide the motivation students need to repeat them on a regular basis. What right do we have to 'expect high standards' as a school, if there is no recognition given when students meet these high standards day in and day out?

Interactions

Just as children need to have positive feedback on the things they do, they also require this same feedback on how they behave with others.

It is important to be conscious of the fact that children and young people can learn just as much about themselves and how they should treat people from their negative interactions as they do from their positive interactions. Conflict is inevitable and when it occurs, the adults must model how that conflict is resolved. It is worth reinforcing the importance of equipping young people with the skills to deal with conflict from an early age. A child who flourishes does so confident in the knowledge that hurdles such as conflict may well be just around the corner, but is secure in the knowledge that they have the skills to manage such inevitabilities.

Achievements

Schools are usually highly effective when it comes to recognising the achievements of their students. The traditional milestones exist in most schools, whether those are sports days, school reports, parent evenings, awards evenings, house points or a system of certificates for attendance, progress or academic performance.

Inclusive schools, which aim to support and celebrate the diverse needs and achievements of all students, use a wider variety of reward systems to ensure that all children feel valued and recognised. These reward systems go beyond traditional academic achievements to include social, emotional and behavioural growth, as well as contributions to the school community. A school that enables students to flourish also considers the following:

- **Personalised learning goals**: achievements are based on the individual's milestones rather than competitive ones.
- **Positive behaviour**: based on interactions and actions with others and linked to the school's values and the personal targets of the child.
- **Citizenship awards**: recognising kindness, leadership and positive citizenship skills and behaviours.
- **Growth mindset recognition**: recognising how a student responds to, and overcomes, challenges.
- **Club and community involvement**: recognising involvement in extra-curricular activities (ECAs), teams and school life 'beyond the classroom'.
- **Class rewards**: designed to build a greater sense of community and to encourage teamwork to achieve collective goals and targets.

There should be a clear path for all students in a class (indeed, a school) to achieve and be recognised for their achievements based on their own targets and stage of development. The importance of achievement in school extends beyond the classroom. It is a multifaceted approach that should include academic success, personal growth, social and emotional development, and the unlocking and mastery of essential life skills. By developing a culture that values and supports all forms of achievement, schools can create environments where every student has the opportunity to thrive and achieve their full potential.

> ## ASIDE
>
> This very brief summary of flourishing would be disingenuous if we did not acknowledge that, like 'happiness', there are many barriers that exist which may prevent a child from being able to flourish. We have already touched upon the importance of inclusive educational practices to ensure that school environments provide pathways for *all* students to thrive in their environment.
>
> Beyond the school itself, there are increasing socioeconomic factors, including child poverty, domestic violence and neglect as well as the absence of parental support and involvement, that may negatively impact a child's ability to flourish. While there is little that we can do as educators to mitigate these challenges, it is still possible, within the confines of the school day and environment, for a child to flourish in our care, despite these very damaging circumstances in which they find themselves beyond school. Mental health and physical health issues will also present their own challenges when we look to enable children to flourish, but it can be done. It is, perhaps, one of the most rewarding achievements for those who work with children disadvantaged in these ways when they thrive, despite their challenges, because the school has created the conditions to enable them to do so.

Points for reflection:

- If you divided all your interactions with students into positive and negative, which would come out on top?
- What is most important to you and the other teachers in your school: students following rules or students being provided with opportunities to flourish?
- How are your learning activities and schemes of work designed with flourishing in mind?
- How is the acquisition of new skills celebrated in your classroom?
- Is it more important that the work is completed or that the students feel good about themselves for working towards a new skill?
- Do you know which students in your class are flourishing, which are coping and which are languishing? What is being done to support those who are languishing?

GRATITUDE

Full disclosure: Gratitude is my favourite wellbeing word in this A–Z list. Yet despite all sorts of books having been written on the subject, gratitude remains an overlooked and misunderstood black sheep in the wellbeing family. The science behind gratitude is a fascinating area of research that explores the psychological, physiological and social impact of practising gratitude. Several studies have provided insights into the mechanisms through which gratitude influences wellbeing (Manuel, 2022).

It is no surprise that the act of showing gratitude and being grateful is a concept that is as old as time itself. It is promoted widely in most religions, perhaps the earliest documented acknowledgement of the innate links that exist between gratitude, faith and personal growth. The science, which now backs up the claims of the benefits of gratitude, has given way to something of a rebirth in modern thinking around how gratitude can be harnessed to enhance wellbeing and it is so much more than just saying 'thank you'. The science certainly gives it gravitas beyond the simple act of showing appreciation through manners and platitudes.

NEUROLOGICAL CHANGES

Research now suggests that practising gratitude can lead to changes in the brain, particularly in areas associated with reward, empathy and social bonding. The prefrontal cortex, which is involved in decision-making and emotional regulation, is often implicated in gratitude studies. Increasingly, wellbeing-focused schools are starting to champion gratitude as a wellbeing 'game changer' as well as a 'brain changer' to celebrate and hype up its impact. Wellbeing journals can help students track success, challenges and changes to their mood, as practising gratitude is introduced and then starts to become second nature.

NEUROTRANSMITTERS

Gratitude has been linked to the release of neurotransmitters like dopamine and serotonin, that play crucial roles in mood regulation. Increased levels of these neurotransmitters are associated with feelings of happiness and can positively impact wellbeing. It is important to have students reflect on how they feel after practising gratitude so those 'feel good' neurotransmitters are firing and get the recognition they deserve. This also helps embed the practice outside of the classroom.

Talking about gratitude at the start or the end of the day and reflecting on the process and its impact is as important as the act itself. How do students feel when they are shown gratitude and how does it feel to be grateful to others? Both are very important conversations to have.

HORMONAL EFFECTS

Gratitude has been shown to increase levels of oxytocin, often referred to as the 'bonding hormone'. Oxytocin is associated with social bonding, trust and positive social interactions. In a school or classroom environment, there is potential to use gratitude to help strengthen relationships by creating moments where students can give positive feedback to one another at the end of a school day or on completion of a project, or after a performance, speech or activity.

Make it a standard part of the evaluation process whenever students work in pairs or groups to take time out to recognise the contribution of others as a way of practising gratitude. You may find engagement improves as a result.

PSYCHOLOGICAL WELLBEING

Engaging in gratitude practices is linked to increased positive emotions such as joy, happiness and contentment. Grateful individuals often report higher life satisfaction and a more optimistic outlook on life. Being in the habit of regularly showing gratitude requires a shift in mindset for some young people and, like any new habit, nothing beats regular practice! Remember that not all students will be confident enough to do this verbally at the start. Drop boxes, Google Forms, Padlets and sticky notes are all acceptable alternatives to verbal and face-to-face practices to begin with, but these are less impactful than verbal feedback and should only be used to get students into the habit before moving on to verbal feedback.

PHYSICAL HEALTH

Gratitude practices have been associated with lower levels of stress. Chronic stress has a detrimental effect on both physical and mental health, and gratitude may serve as a protective factor against stress-related disorders. When involved in a behavioural incident or when dealing with an upset student, being calm in highly emotive environments can de-escalate situations and prevent things from escalating further.

Modelling gratitude is a cunning diversion tactic that can be employed to manage the drama that might be unfolding and cuts off the supply line to the tension and angst the child might be feeling. Even in the midst of upset, gratitude can still be practised.

> 'I really appreciate how honest you are being with me about this. How does that make you feel?'
>
> 'How kind was that of Kavita to bring you to my office so we could sort this out? When we find her later, what would you like to say to her?'
>
> 'You reacted very maturely when Mrs Fearn asked you to leave the playground. This really helped her to stop the fight. What might have happened if you hadn't followed her orders, do you think?'

This positive affirmation style of questioning places the focus back on the desirable aspects of the student's behaviour and emotions and helps reduce stress.

SOCIAL EFFECTS

Expressing gratitude encourages positive social behaviour and can help strengthen social bonds. Grateful individuals tend to be more supportive and responsive in their relationships, creating a positive feedback loop of social connection. They are more accepting and tolerant of others and empathise more readily.

Ask the students in your class: 'Can you remember the last time someone told you they were grateful and appreciative of something you had said or done?'. There is a lot to learn about the wellbeing climate in your class/school by their responses and the frequency with which this takes place. Whether part of an explicit restorative practice approach, or simply rebuilding relationships between students in conflict, asking children to show appreciation of the other person is a great way to start a dialogue around a conflict or fallout. It reframes, it reduces stress and it de-escalates, setting a more appreciative tone for the rest of the discussion.

COGNITIVE EFFECTS

Gratitude practices often involve reflecting on the positive aspects of a person's life. This shift in perspective can contribute to a healthier mindset, helping individuals focus on what they *have* rather than what they *want*. This is seen most explicitly following tragedies, disasters and death.

Apply this logic to the perennial moaners in the staffroom. You know the ones – every staffroom has them. Imagine if they could just take a breath and look upwards through the periscope of positivity once in a while and remember the small mercies we are oft reminded to be grateful for: having a job, a roof over one's head, food on the table and a lovely half-term holiday to look forward to in a couple of weeks' time. There are plenty of people worse off and having a pile of marking and an inbox full of emails is, after all, just part of the job.

If a child or an adult is genuinely unable to name anything they are grateful for, appreciative of or looking forward to, it should ring alarm bells around their own wellbeing or mental health, as this can be an indicator of more serious underlying issues or indicate they are 'stuck' in a trauma or mindset they need professional help coming out of.

BEHAVIOURAL CHANGES

Grateful individuals are more likely to engage in behaviours that benefit others. This may include acts of kindness, cooperation and altruism. When the neurotransmitters are firing on all cylinders, it can become mildly addictive so we find ways to keep those rewards coming. Like physical training after a period of slovenly behaviour (think Christmas and the New Year health kick), it can seem a chore at first, but once the habit has formed, it becomes the norm and improvements in wellbeing are noticeable as the feel-good factor kicks in and we reap the mental rewards.

In your classroom, reward acts of gratitude, particularly those that are spontaneous and organic beyond the teaching of gratitude. Ensure students are not just showing gratitude purely for the rewards, though; that should not be the motivating factor.

RESILIENCE

Gratitude has been identified as a coping mechanism that enhances resilience in the face of adversity. Grateful individuals can often be better equipped to navigate challenges and setbacks. Celebrate stories of successful people who have had to show resilience in their journey. You can usually guarantee that they have also shown immense gratitude along the way for those who have helped and supported them. Any Oscar acceptance speech is evidence of that!

SLEEP IMPROVEMENT

Some research studies suggest that practising gratitude may contribute to improved sleep quality. Grateful individuals often report better sleep patterns and duration. Ending the day recording gratitude in a journal emphasises the positives that have been a feature of the day, leading to a more content and relaxed state ahead of going to bed.

When gratitude becomes an accepted part of the class or school culture, it spreads and grows. Practise it in the staffroom too. I know of one school that has a tradition that the morning staff briefing always ends with a 'Golden Apple' award. The recipient of the award holds it for a week before nominating another colleague to receive it for a kind act, for going above and beyond or for simply being a supportive and valued colleague. What a great way to start the day – to be part of a staffroom that shows gratitude and appreciation in this way.

> ## ASIDE
>
> Gratitude, when misunderstood, done poorly or implemented without a real understanding of the concept, can be cringeworthy to observe. Gratitude is more than just manners and remembering to say 'please' and 'thank you'; it is a fundamental awareness and appreciation of the people, places, opportunities and environments around us all.
>
> In schools not blessed with the wealth of resources afforded to most, such as many of the rural township schools in South Africa, it is common to find that, despite the schools having almost no resources (and sometimes no electricity), the pupils are full of gratitude for being in school and receiving an education. It is a humbling experience to work with pupils who require little more than a teacher's time, patience and expertise.
>
> Gratitude should not just exist on a material level, which is sometimes how it is reinforced in young people, especially by parents. Appreciation of beauty, for example, is a wonderful character strength and falls under the virtue of gratitude because it grounds us when we use it to be reminded of our place in the world and all that it has to offer. Those who are blessed with this character strength find moments in the day to appreciate what they see as beautiful around them. It could be as simple as the wind creating ripples of waves in the grass or as impressive as the awesome impact of a tidal storm. It is certainly not for us to judge a child on what they find beautiful; children often see beauty in things that most adults have stopped bothering to notice. The impact on wellbeing is almost instant as that moment of beauty brings clarity and reassurance back to the anxious or wandering mind.

GRATITUDE

1. Practising gratitude is best placed at the start or the end of the school day or individual lessons, as it gives students the opportunity to positively reframe their mindset.
2. At the start, students may not wish to say aloud what they are grateful for. Allow it to be a private moment of reflection for students who don't yet feel confident enough to share.
3. Ensure students can access different aspects of their life to show gratitude for: people, places, moments, feelings, interactions, belongings, pets and future plans are all prompts to get students reflecting.
4. Model gratitude, make it explicit and reward students when they practise it without prompting.
5. Make it a staff practice. Try not to let a day go by where you don't express gratitude to someone you work with. It will become part of the culture.

HAPPINESS

If you ask any parent what they want for their kids, the words 'healthy' and 'happy' should always be battling it out for the top spot, and rightly so. Academic achievements, grades and progress in school should be further down the list of priorities.

Unfortunately, happiness and wellbeing are often used in an interchangeable way. With the increased prevalence and emphasis of 'wellbeing' as a term in education, some can find the difference between the two too subtle to observe. There is some overlap, but while wellbeing is more concerned with the broader quality of our life, happiness is an emotion that comes from experiencing pleasure, joy or contentment.

In many respects, 'wellbeing' risks becoming something of a dirty word if we fall into the trap of reducing it or equating it to a child's temporary level of happiness. Teachers themselves have spoken about the burden of pressure that comes with being responsible for a pupil's happiness because, for starters, how do you even measure such a thing?

This is not to say that there is no quantifiable link between the concepts of 'happiness' and 'wellbeing' because, of course, there is. The problems occur when the rich soup of ingredients that make up wellbeing is watered down to an over-simplified base. There are two types of happiness: hedonic and eudaimonic.

- **Hedonic happiness** can be obtained through pleasure and enjoyment and is usually temporary or the shorter-lived of the two types.
- **Eudaimonic happiness** is experienced through deeper meaning, accomplishment and purpose.

Psychologists believe that both types of happiness are important for a person to flourish and schools are places where the conditions are perfect for students to experience both of these daily. So, what is the problem with happiness?

The problem involves the fundamental misunderstanding of 'wellbeing' as a concept. When we stand up in front of parents at open days and curriculum evenings and talk about the school's commitment to the wellbeing of our pupils, it should always come with a disclaimer that this does not mean that the children will not experience difficulties, unhappiness and stressful moments. Indeed, a school that is serious about wellbeing will embrace such moments as opportunities to reinforce and develop a child's resilience to promote deeper, more authentic and transformational wellbeing in the longer term.

'Unhappiness', and how these moments are managed and overcome, is sometimes the more painful route to genuine and sustained wellbeing. As teachers, leaders and parents, our instinct is to protect and shield our children from harm; in response to any upset or trauma, we seek to 'fix' things as quickly as possible. In this quest for hedonic happiness, we often burn several potential eudaimonic bridges in the process.

When a school's headteacher asked for feedback on their recent focus on student wellbeing, and how it was being implemented by their staff, they were surprised by the response given by the inspectors. In one class, the inspectors observed a QR code that was used to direct students to a photo of a page from the textbook (that was already open in front of the students). When asked about this, the teacher said, 'It was good for the students' wellbeing to use their devices. It made them happy.' In another class, the teacher wrapped up the lesson five minutes early and then dutifully handed out a biscuit to each student. The students then ate the biscuit in silence while classical music was played over the interactive whiteboard. 'Why?', the teacher was asked afterwards. 'Student wellbeing' was the proud reply.

When we dilute wellbeing to such arbitrary processes, it serves only to confuse the entire community about the purpose and aims of what should be a more meaningful approach to student wellbeing. Neither of these strategies had anything to do with wellbeing. They were simply a teacher's interpretation of what would make the pupils happy in the short term.

Happiness should not be a goal state. For some people, happiness may never be achieved, so to be dangling this as a target, out of reach for some, could actually be damaging. Instead, we should be talking about how we create the conditions in our schools for students to flourish and thrive. We should normalise and be accepting of the times when students are unhappy, and provide them with the tools they need to lift themselves from this state to a more comfortable emotive and mental position – which does not necessarily need to be happiness.

Wellbeing is often misconstrued as being something that is affected and impacted by others. It can be, of course, but the starting point for any successful and purposeful wellbeing programme is to acknowledge and empower individuals to be the drivers of their own wellbeing first and foremost. When we devolve the responsibility onto others, we lose the most powerful tool we have: agency. Not all children are born with this autonomy; it has to be taught and developed like any other skill. When we remove all the barriers and pitfalls for them, we are incorrectly modelling that life is easy.

A PLACE FOR HEDONIC HAPPINESS?

Yes, of course! What would life be like if we did not have the glorious boosts of happiness afforded to us in these moments?

Schools can be tough places at times and we are all human after all! A teacher new to a school was amazed that the pupils asked every lesson if they could watch a film. As an English teacher, it is not completely out of the question that the use of media might be part of a learning activity, but the frequency and clamour for every lesson to be a movie lesson felt strange to the teacher. When it was raised with the head of department, it was revealed that the last teacher of this class struggled with behaviour management and the promise of being able to watch a film was the only way they could get the class to engage.

That teacher relied solely upon hedonic happiness to get the class through the lesson and, of course, the teenage students lapped it up and took full advantage of this teacher's weakness and willingness to get them onboard by making them happy. But, did it really make them happy? Not at all, it simply delayed the eventual effort and energy they would be asked to apply to their learning in the other lessons they went to that day.

Another example, away from teaching, of someone who completely misunderstood the role of the different types of happiness and wellbeing, is David Brent from the hit TV sitcom 'The Office' (or his American counterpart Michael Scott, if you prefer the US version).

These characters were terrible at their jobs, but they fell into the trap of believing they were effective leaders because they thought that their use of humour, a lax approach to discipline and the fact that they promoted and instilled a poor work ethic among their teams made them popular. Teachers are all leaders, and as leaders we make unpopular decisions for the long-term benefit of our students. Not every learning moment is a happy moment. Not every school day can be full of joy. The rewards should come through positive relationships, the acquisition of new skills and a sense of belonging.

There is nothing wrong with planned or spontaneous moments of hedonic happiness, provided these exist alongside a sequenced and strategic wellbeing programme. After all, these moments help build relationships between teachers and pupils, especially when used as a reward or an incentive. However, if students are taught that wellbeing is only achieved through temporary moments of pleasure, then a deeper understanding and appreciation of resilience and how to thrive cannot co-exist, especially in younger children.

Parents, too, can use wellbeing as a stick to beat you with in the absence of understanding of how wellbeing progresses along a continuum. No doubt we have all had the email or the phone call from the upset parent informing us that their child was called names in the playground last week and how it has impacted their 'wellbeing', despite the school's promise of promoting positive wellbeing. Parents will also need support and guidance to understand and appreciate that it is through the teaching of the skills needed to manage such behaviours that wellbeing will be achieved for the child in the long term.

There is no shortcut to genuine wellbeing and the belief that children who are outwardly happy can also be considered as being 'well' is flawed.

The child who is outwardly happy at school may present as such because home is such an unhappy place in contrast. Likewise, the child who is outwardly unhappy at school is going to receive no long-term benefit to his wellbeing by being allowed to skip numeracy that morning and play with Lego in the home corner instead. He is only going to learn that challenges can be delayed if you play the teacher in the right way.

> # ASIDE
>
> It is natural that, as adults who have chosen to work with children, we want to see happiness in our schools and classrooms. As long as we understand happiness as an emotion and wellbeing as a state, we can avoid the problematic interchange of the two concepts.
>
> Consider the following two questions which were asked as a plenary at the end of the school day by a school trialling wellbeing practices. Notice how the replies are significantly different, with the wellbeing answers being far more valuable. One has happiness as the subject while the other uses the term wellbeing.
>
> **What made you *happy* today?**
>
> There were chicken nuggets in the tuck shop.
>
> I don't have a swimming lesson after school.
>
> My friend was back in today after being off ill.
>
> Mr X was absent. I don't like Mr X.
>
> I didn't get any homework.
>
> **What helped your *wellbeing* today?**
>
> You asking us how we are all feeling today.
>
> I finished my project, even though I found it hard.
>
> I feel more optimistic about my university personal statement now.
>
> Someone I fell out with apologised.

The difference in the responses is clear. When the focus was on wellbeing, students were reflective and offered responses that pertained to longer-term benefits/changes. This was very different from the responses from those who focused only on their happiness. The responses to the happiness question only highlighted temporary and superficial differences to their day that would be unlikely to result in longer-term outcomes for their wellbeing.

1. Having a shared grammar around wellbeing is essential. Ensure students know the difference between wellbeing and happiness so they don't confuse one for the other.
2. Ensure challenges, problems, difficulties and conflict are a normalised experience that sits within your strategy for wellbeing. Use these as learning points and ensure parents are clear that your strategy does not seek to eradicate these from the lives of their children.
3. 'Peardeck' users may be familiar with an activity that asks students to name something that is 'filling their bucket' and something that is 'draining it'. As well as being a gratitude exercise, this is a great way to signpost what is positively contributing to a child's wellbeing and what is contributing to their happiness.
4. Talk to students about a wellbeing continuum. Use terms like languishing, thriving, flourishing, content and stable to describe the differences in emotions that exist between the extreme ends of that continuum.
5. Don't throw out activities or events that are done purely to create moments of joy. They are special in the eyes of your students.

ILLBEING

Illbeing is not a term or concept that is used with much frequency. It is an umbrella term that captures all the aspects of a person's physical, mental and emotional conditions that prevent them from being 'well'. Just as 'wellbeing' can seem too broad for some, the same can be said for 'illbeing'.

As teachers, we would be more likely to refer to a pupil not being 'well'. Furthermore, the use of 'ill' has primary connotations of physical illness and describing someone as being 'mentally ill' is no longer appropriate. However, as a person's wellbeing operates along a continuum, it is important to acknowledge and understand what contributes to someone being unable to experience positive wellbeing when they are positioned at the negative end of the wellbeing continuum.

Identifying these signs in a child or young adult can be difficult. We are, after all, neither doctors nor mental health professionals. But with our knowledge of each child's usual traits, habits and behaviours, we are often in a much stronger position than most adults to raise concerns that may enable the correct professionals to intervene further. We are all, to some extent as teachers, first-aiders – physically, emotionally and behaviourally. The role of a first-aider is to preserve life before the arrival of the experts and we are usually the first on the scene.

PHYSICAL

The physical health of a child can often be the easiest condition to assess visually, as some of the signs of physical illness are difficult to disguise. Broken bones, cuts, bruises, scrapes and scratches are all a part of growing up and the rough-and-tumble nature of childhood. These alone do not always point to illbeing or abuse, but this should never be ruled out. For example, the girl who was embarrassed about the cuts on her arms told her school nurse they were caused by her cat. The switched-on school nurse correctly raised the alarm knowing that cats don't scratch in uniform straight lines and the girl received the help she needed.

Likewise, the boy who told his teacher that his broken arm was caused by a fall from a swing one week, then changing it to a fall from a *bike* the next. The boy unknowingly raised the alarm; the observant teacher reported this to the designated safeguarding lead (DSL) and abuse at home was uncovered.

Another example is that of the teacher of a particular child who was concerned that they were always ill with various stomach aches, viral infections, sickness and bugs. The teacher raised the issue in that week's pastoral meeting. A home visit found her to be living in squalid, mouldy conditions and the authorities were able to intervene before her health got even worse.

These are extremes, but each example shows the importance of the adult in monitoring, assessing and taking action. Alongside these physical manifestations of ill health, great wellbeing practice requires us to be mindful of a pupil's personal hygiene, sleep hygiene, changes in appetite and energy levels/fatigue. Reporting and recording concerns on your school's dedicated wellbeing platform or management information system (MIS) is essential in helping the pastoral team or DSL build a picture of how these physical concerns may prevent a more serious decline in a pupil's wellbeing.

EMOTIONAL

Regardless of the age of the pupils you are working with, you are dealing with emotional and sensitive beings every day you are in school. While emotional signs of illbeing can sometimes be as visual as the physical signs, children can be very skilled and adept at hiding signs of emotional distress. It is equally difficult for both new and experienced teachers to decide whether the mood swings experienced by those in their class are hormonal/puberty related, or whether something more concerning is at play.

The same can be said for the anxious child who may still be able to thrive and flourish in spite of the difficulties their condition can bring them at times. With anxiety in children on the rise, it is ever more incumbent on schools who prioritise wellbeing to ensure teachers are trained to spot the signs of anxiety and offer basic psychological first aid and coping strategies to alleviate those moments of increased stress and worry. Finally, low self-esteem, persistent sadness and worry, particularly as home time approaches, can all be signs that intervention is needed and not merely dismissed as just a normal part of growing up.

Children experience intense emotions as they grow and develop. These emotions can often be overwhelming and difficult to manage without support and guidance. Encouraging a culture where a pupil can talk about their emotions with someone they trust is advice that appears frequently when we consider a child's wellbeing, because it is so essential. It is not easy for a child to discuss some of these emotions, especially those which they may be experiencing for the first time: a crush, romantic feelings, a broken heart, jealousy, loss/grief. These are incredibly sensitive and private emotions and should be treated as such at all times.

In the absence of a loving, kind and trusting family unit, where we would hope these feelings could be addressed and explored, the school may be the only safe place a child has to articulate and understand these emotions without having them suppressed or avoided altogether.

BEHAVIOUR

It is worth re-emphasising briefly here just how important it is to understand the complexities and context of a child's behaviour and the implications this has for us all as teachers, leaders and as members of school communities.

Those who work with pre-teens and adolescents perhaps find themselves in the least enviable position as they try to navigate the fine line that exists between changes in behaviour that are hormonal and changes in behaviour that are signs that the student needs help and support. These changes are not always necessarily extreme or easy to observe. Withdrawal, for example, can occur over a period of weeks or months and may be a natural part of the student's development from childhood into adolescence. Where that withdrawal seems to be centred around the avoidance of social situations or increasingly feeling uncomfortable around others, it may be advisable to try to better understand what is causing these feelings and what support the student needs before this develops into a potentially more serious condition that impacts on their wellbeing.

The teacher who values a pupil's wellbeing will look at behaviour through a wellbeing lens, rather than a punitive one, as they constantly assess and monitor each pupil in their care. When we reframe our thinking away from 'poor behaviour must = sanctions' to 'poor behaviour could = an unmet need', we are better placed to support and nurture our young people.

ASIDE

Teachers deal with students not being 'well' on a daily basis. So frequent are our interactions with illbeing that we often accept or dismiss it as a normal part of a child's life, and, to a large extent, it is. Raising concerns about a child's health can often be met with some resistance or even cause offence to parents, which is why it is important that any action is taken following consultation with school leaders and those with pastoral responsibility.

Some questions you might ask yourself:

1. Is the reason for the child's injury valid and consistent?
2. Are the injuries sustained in places children normally experience injuries from regular falls, collisions, scrapes and play? (Knees, shins, hands/palms, elbows, feet, chin, forehead — these are usual 'impact' points and joints that can suffer injury.)
3. How has that child sustained an injury in places less likely to be affected by, for example, a fall, such as the back, inner thighs, upper/inner arms, stomach, cheeks and eyes? These are usually 'soft flesh' areas that don't generally suffer impact from a regular fall or bump.

4. Does the child's change in mood coincide with any changes in the family context that you are (or aren't) aware of?
5. If sensitive questions need to be asked of the child, who is best placed to do that? It may not always be you. Who do they trust the most? Who is most experienced to do it in a way that is not intrusive and that will not cause alarm to the child?
6. What purpose is the sanction you are going to impose on the child going to serve? Will it impact positively or negatively on the underlying symptoms that caused them to behave that way?
7. Is the child's illness indicative of a wider concern about their overall wellbeing, or is it simply an isolated and unfortunate bout of ill health?
8. What information might other teachers/adults in the school have about this child and their family that may help you better understand the concern I have about them?

JENGA

The 'Jenga' tower goes through three physical states during the course of a game: stability, instability and collapse. Once the tower is toppled, the game can only begin again by rebuilding the tower, brick by brick, layer by layer. It would be impossible to play the game with – let's say – just three layers of the wooden bricks. The tower would be too simple and too solid to be toppled. The foundations would be so secure with just the three levels on their own, it would take all the fun out of the game.

When we consider why wellbeing programmes can fail in schools, we might consider this analogy of the game Jenga. Upon initial construction, the tower of blocks is completely stable. Gradually, as blocks are taken away from their stable foundations, layered on top of pre-existing blocks, often added on with little care or at an awkward angle, the once-stable tower starts to lose its integrity. It becomes lopsided, cannot handle any more layers and, ultimately, topples over completely, resulting in the tower needing to be rebuilt from scratch.

This analogy proposes that the leadership of student wellbeing has followed a very similar model of growth and instability in the last few years. Whereas we once relied on the most fundamental concepts – such as relationships, school culture and teacher wellbeing – as the basis for positive student wellbeing, in the post-Covid haste to become better informed and more sophisticated in our approach to wellbeing, we have layered on more and more expectations of teachers in terms of their knowledge and practices, resulting in instability and overload.

If the Jenga tower was a physical manifestation of student wellbeing, we would be blessed with the simplicity offered by three levels of 'bricks'.

The foundations of student wellbeing, starting from these simple, stable levels would consist of:

1. strong and positive relationships in school between staff and students
2. a school culture that can support a meaningful wellbeing programme
3. a genuine focus on teacher wellbeing.

These three levels offer a stable base that can support the tower as it continues to build. Without these in place, or if they have been poorly established, anything added to this base is in danger of causing instability. Yet this is exactly what many schools did in the post-Covid rush to 'do wellbeing well'. We added in complex science, changed our language, sought accreditation, increased our expectations on class teachers, spent money on 'off the shelf' wellbeing programmes/ applications and all of these extra 'bricks' or layers toppled the tower for many schools.

Some schools have fallen victim to the simple mistake of trying to do 'too much, too quick'. Which is not to criticise or discourage those schools. After all, Covid shook us all to the core, especially as our approaches to wellbeing and mental health were thrust under the spotlight, unfairly in most cases, as no one could have predicted the speed at which the profession was forced to respond to a global lockdown and the impact this would have on our students, families and communities.

The schools that were so effective at wellbeing pre-Covid found that they were hit the hardest. Schools where relationships between staff and students had previously been strong suffered when those relationships were interrupted and forced into the strange and detached world of online teaching.

Schools that had a strong culture of wellbeing in place found their students suffered when they could no longer physically access the support from the school's positive and supportive culture. Schools that prioritised and excelled in practices around staff wellbeing found that the lack of a staffroom, face-to-face communication, social events, line-management structure and just the general care and kindness afforded from one professional to another resulted in staff who felt isolated and bereft in the absence of such a wonderfully warm working environment.

Equally, many schools found it hard to slip back into the old rhythm when their schools reopened, particularly with social distancing and all the other Covid restrictions, making schools feel slightly alien, even dystopian, compared to how students remembered their school experiences pre-Covid.

As schools reopened after lockdowns, the race was on to rebuild the 'Jenga' wellbeing tower, but many schools took the basics for granted, particularly if they had previously excelled in these areas. We had no idea what impact the lockdowns had had on students and we were optimistic (or naïve) enough to assume that relationships, culture and teacher wellbeing could resume, as if they had been on pause all this time, unaffected upon our return to the classroom. School leaders, especially, responded by pursuing wellbeing courses, speakers and programmes to try to ensure that any impact of the lockdown/pandemic could be handled effectively and efficiently.

Schools are increasingly marketing themselves with their wellbeing specialisms and expertise as a selling point. Parents are now looking at how a school prioritises wellbeing with as much attention as grades and other academic metrics as society places increased emphasis on how a child is nurtured in addition to the quality of teaching and learning.

Ofsted reports, too, have an increased focus on the quality of relationships, behaviour, wellbeing education and teacher wellbeing as part of their assessment criteria. A school cannot pull the wool over the eyes of its students, parents, staff or inspectors when it comes to the integration of genuinely meaningful and transformational wellbeing practices.

It is the role of everyone working with children and young people in a school to ensure that those three basic building blocks of the tower – relationships, culture and teacher wellbeing – are securely embedded. Without these, it becomes increasingly difficult to develop more complex and sophisticated wellbeing practices and strategies.

THE A–Z OF STUDENT WELLBEING

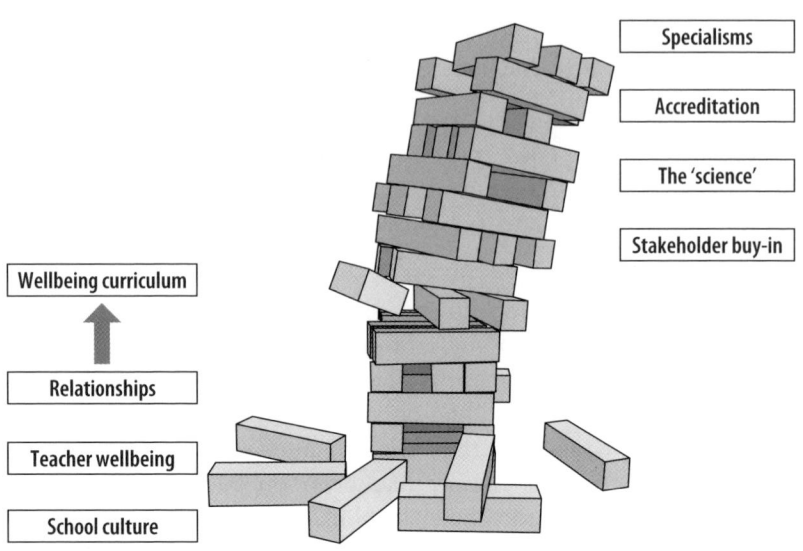

ASIDE

Case study

When was the last time your school undertook an audit of its culture? Some schools outsource this task to specialist external agencies, because the complexities and biases that can occur from such a task can be too overwhelming when managing it in-house.

One school had clearly not done this due diligence before implementing their new, shiny wellbeing programme and bringing in an inspector to assess it.

Before even taking a look at the programme, the inspector asked to meet with a group of students and a group of staff. Within an hour, it was clear that this programme was doomed to fail. The students gave at least a dozen reasons why they did not feel that the school took wellbeing seriously. The inspector believed them. The staff they met with readily pointed out the school's last inspection report where wellbeing was highly criticised.

> The programme implemented by this school was nothing but a quick fix; a sticking plaster to cover more fundamental problems around relationships and culture. The school was reluctant to rebuild the 'Jenga' tower from scratch and, as a result, the programme failed within six months because neither staff nor students believed in it.
>
> If you have the opportunity to conduct an audit of your wellbeing provision, there are some simple questions you can use as a starting point given in Section Two, pages 173–174.

KNOWLEDGE

It has almost become a societal norm to demonise and denigrate the younger generation. Most generations of young adults over the last century have been vilified for a behaviour or trait not understood by their 'elders'. Rock and roll music was the scourge of the 1960s and was seen as a threat to the wholesome Christian societies those greasy rock and rollers came from. Likewise, the brief spell in the 1970s during which punk rockers shocked and spat their way through a very gloomy, broken Britain sparked concerns about the fabric of society being permanently dismantled.

In more recent times, 'hoodies' and 'chavs' scared the life out of anyone wanting to use their corner shop after dark in the 1990s, and now we apparently have a generation of gamers and social-media addicts who live their lives online and perish in the presence of daylight or at the thought of face-to-face social interaction.

> 'They disrespect their elders, they disobey their parents, they ignore the law. They riot in the streets inflamed with wild notions.'
>
> Attributed to Plato

We have been underestimating and berating children and young people since the very earliest thinkers, such as Plato, began putting pen to papyrus. This phenomenon of demonising kids can be explained by the fact that each new generation purposely aim to exhibit traits, habits and behaviours that clearly distinguish them from their parents' generation.

As I type this, my own teenage children are blaring indecipherable rap music from their bedrooms, despite the fact I raised them on a diet of 'proper' music, such as Oasis, Blur and Ocean Colour Scene. And therein lies the exact problem: too many adults, including those in education, hold children and young people to the same standards, expectations and norms they experienced in their formative years, without any acknowledgement that the world is a very different place from the one we grew up in all those years ago.

The fact that most children do not want to grow up exactly the same as their parents should not be taken as a sign of disrespect. A young person's identity is formed in some way by their rejection of the trends, fashions and wider culture handed down to them by their 'elders'. This is a positive thing as it leads to a creative reimagining of culture as each generation develops their own collective identity.

YOUTHSPEAK

To have some knowledge, interest or appreciation of what it means to be a child or young person in today's society puts a teacher at a distinct advantage when it comes to understanding how to better promote the wellbeing of those in their care. Teachers with children of their own already live a life where this knowledge is constantly being absorbed. The language used by children evolves quicker than ever before as social media enables language trends to spread globally within a matter of days or by a few memes. The lexicon shared by young people can often alienate adults, such is its complexity.

This is even more true when it comes to 'text speak'. The abbreviations, acronyms and emojis used online and on social media are a language of their own, and trends and popularity of slang change on a weekly basis. Should teachers be fluent in this 'youthspeak'? Not at all, though with any foreign language, a little to help you 'get by' with the locals often goes a long way to make communication a little easier. Children will usually be happy to explain to you the meaning of the latest meme, fad or phrase. It is reassuring as an adult to know that the latest fashionable saying has no offensive or sinister meaning when you are hearing it traded across the classroom or around the playground. It can also be quite bewildering when you use a word in its usual form, only to find out – through the response of the class – that it now has a secondary usage understood only by those of a certain age.

Take, for example, the unfortunate moment during a lesson observation where a female maths teacher made an innocuous joke about herself not being 'thick' in terms of her intelligence. Both the teacher and the observing assistant head were surprised by the response of the class which was a mixture of hilarity and embarrassment until one kindly student informed the confused adults that to be 'thicc', for a woman, meant being full-figured or voluptuous, particularly in relation to the lady's bottom! A lesson learned for the slightly bemused staff, though by the time you read this, the word will already be out of circulation, or 'cringe' as the kids would say.

SOCIAL MEDIA

If you have a pastoral responsibility in your school, it is becoming increasingly important that you have a proficient level of social-media literacy. It can be difficult to understand an incident or complaint where some of the behaviour has taken place online (as is often the case) if the teacher or leader investigating the situation has little knowledge of the main social-media platforms. Children and young people will purposely migrate to social-media apps and platforms unfamiliar to adults, which means that your fluency in WhatsApp is unlikely to be of use in the online space inhabited by children.

Facebook, for example, is now populated mainly by adults aged 40+. Young people, especially teens, do not want to hang out digitally in the same spaces as their aunts, uncles, grandmas and grandads, especially if they want to be their ideal 'teenage' self and not the little kiddies their family members treat them as. Having a working knowledge of Snapchat, TikTok, Discord, Instagram, etc. will go a long way to helping you better understand online behaviours that may be affecting a student's wellbeing.

Sadly, just being able to navigate the app may not be sufficient to help you understand what may have caused the issue. Each app has its own set of codes and expectations. Being *added* or *removed* from a group, being *left undelivered*, *following* and *unfollowing*, *public/private* accounts, Snap *scores*, *streaks* and *best friends* all carry varying amounts of social currency. Adherence to, or deviation from, the rules of maintaining relationships on these apps can be a source of reassurance or conflict which, to the digital non-native, can be almost impossible to understand without the correct knowledge.

Fortunately, there are plenty of resources available online to help you understand each of these platforms and you could not find a better starting point for such resources than the National College which has a fully comprehensive library of resources, videos, courses and infographics covering every app, website or game your pupils are likely to encounter.

GAMING

As computers and gaming consoles have developed over the last 40 years, gaming is no longer the sole domain of the young. Gaming is almost as common among adults aged 21–40 as it is in those aged 11–18. The rise in Esports has elevated gaming to a professional level with elite 'gamers' making millions of pounds in prize money and through social-media views, advertisements and endorsements.

Even those teachers coming to the end of their careers are likely to have used some sort of technology in a gaming capacity at some point in their lives, even if this is limited to the odd game of Candy Crush on their phones. Gaming is here to stay and as we continue to understand the positives and negatives around a child's engagement with online gaming, our ability to support the wellbeing of young people can only be enhanced by knowing a little about the pros and cons of what it means to 'game' or be a 'gamer', 'streamer' or 'influencer'.

There are certainly many positives about some aspects of gaming. This, of course, depends on the nature of the game, the child's relationship with the game and adherence to healthy habits. For the purpose of this positive take on the issue, we are only referring to age-appropriate games designed with children and teens in mind such as Minecraft, Roblox, Pokemon, Animal Crossing, etc. and, to some extent, Fortnite (which is advised for teens aged 13+).

Many of these games enhance problem-solving skills and have been shown to have benefits to critical-thinking development and hand–eye coordination. There is a reliance on social interaction and collaboration in many of these games, with young people connecting with their friends using video- and audio-chat facilities. The purpose here is not to convince you that gaming is all positive, but simply suggest that some children do experience an uplift in their wellbeing when they are engaged and connected in this way. Fortunately, for you as the teacher, it is likely that all of this takes place in the home, depending on your school's digital-device policy.

The negatives tend to focus on the addictive nature of these games and the fact that the chat facilities allow strangers online access to our children. Guidance on how many hours a child should spend online varies according to the research and who funded it. Many of these popular games now monetise the ability to advance or succeed in the game through the purchasing of digital currencies such as V-Bucks (Fortnite) and Robux (Roblox). This can be a source of conflict among children in the playground, but also with parents at home.

Children can gain status in a school by being a successful or known gamer, but likewise, taunting or bullying can occur when a child is not as skilled as their classmates. In online worlds such as Minecraft, there have been instances where parents have reported to schools that 'gangs' of other kids from the class have raided their child's online world and blown it to smithereens, causing feelings of trauma and grief at the loss of hours and hours of work spent building it.

ASIDE

Children and young people will naturally relate better with teachers who understand them and their world. We are the adults in the classroom; we are the professionals who lead these schools. Our aim is not to be popular, or to be 'down with the kids', but having some insight and understanding into what makes them tick will enhance our ability to empathise with them and help devise strategies to improve their wellbeing.

1. **Talk to your pupils.** Breaktimes, before school and after school, when learning isn't taking place, are the best times to get to know your class and find out what's in and what's out.
2. **Ask questions.** Don't be embarrassed! You are not supposed to know all the teenage lingo, so don't be afraid to ask what a word or phrase means if it keeps cropping up in class. The vast majority of the time it will be something inoffensive and pointless. Even the most brazen of pupils won't use the really bad slang in class for fear of being exposed.
3. **Ask Google or ChatGPT.** There are lots of websites that will translate youthspeak and text codes, and explain memes to you if you are worried that any of them may be inappropriate, sexual or discriminatory.
4. **Speak to parents.** Find out from them what their children are into, what their online habits are, how long they spend gaming and what restrictions are in place.
5. **Share knowledge and best practice.** Your staffroom is the ultimate resource when it comes to knowledge about children and young people. Parent-teachers have an insight that should be tapped into when needed.

LANGUAGE

Language is the fundamental building block to every interaction in a school, shaping how students think, feel and connect with the world around them. The language used by, and with, children plays a crucial role in their development, self-esteem and overall wellbeing. Their experiences and relationships are affected by the language that is used towards them by the adults and children in their lives.

From the classroom to the playground, the words exchanged can either lift a child up or tear them down – whether intentional or not. Understanding the power of language and how it impacts a pupil's wellbeing is essential for creating a positive, safe and nurturing environment in our schools.

LANGUAGE AND WELLBEING

Language is not just about the transmission of information, it is also very much about emotional expression, relationship building and social inclusion. The words that children hear and use have a direct impact on their self-conceptualisation, confidence and emotional resilience. When used effectively and precisely, language can help children articulate their feelings, resolve conflicts and build healthy relationships that underpin the concepts in almost every chapter we have covered so far.

On the other hand, harmful or inappropriate language can contribute to stress, anxiety, feelings of exclusion and a sense of threat. Children and young people today are increasingly aware of what is and what isn't appropriate in terms of the language that is used around them. The outstanding wellbeing practitioner sets clear boundaries, and outstanding schools have policies, charters or boundaries in place to ensure all staff, students and parents are clear of what is expected when members of the community communicate and interact with one another.

The importance of language in the classroom goes beyond academic instruction, and teachers are skilled in using language precisely to enable learning. How teachers speak to students, whether offering feedback, praise, reprimands or guidance, affects how children view themselves and their place in the world. Positive language fosters an environment where students feel valued, understood and motivated to succeed. It encourages a growth mindset, helping students believe in their ability to improve and learn from mistakes.

In contrast, negative or careless language can undermine a child's confidence and result in them feeling unworthy or incapable. That is not to say that excellent wellbeing practice shies away from conversations that are difficult; language is used carefully and sensitively to tackle these situations from a position of care and compassion, but challenging conversations are as important for wellbeing as the joyous and positive ones.

EMOTIONAL INTELLIGENCE AND LANGUAGE DEVELOPMENT

Language is also a critical tool for emotional expression. From a young age, children must learn and be encouraged to articulate their feelings in healthy, constructive ways. Teachers play a key role in helping students develop emotional literacy, which is the ability to recognise, understand and express their emotions. When children can verbalise their feelings, they are better equipped to navigate emotional challenges and resolve conflicts with peers.

Children who are delayed in their language development, and children who have English as a second language, can sometimes find themselves in conflict more frequently. Not being able to express themselves as clearly or articulately as their peers, and not being understood, can lead to frustration that can manifest itself as a physical or emotional response which, in turn, can lead to behaviour issues.

In schools where emotional language is encouraged, pupils feel more secure in expressing how they feel, knowing that they will be met with empathy and support. For example, encouraging students to use phrases like 'I feel upset because ...', rather than acting out in frustration or apportioning blame, helps them develop emotional regulation and improves social awareness. Teachers can model this behaviour by using language that acknowledges children's emotions, such as 'I can see that you're feeling frustrated. Let's talk about what's bothering you.' This type of language and the openness that it encourages should be standard in a classroom. No child should be denied a voice and all children should be supported in using their voice.

LANGUAGE CHARTERS AND PROTECTING CHILDREN FROM HARMFUL LANGUAGE

One effective way in which schools can foster a positive language environment is by implementing a language charter. A language charter is a community-wide agreement that outlines expectations for respectful and positive communication. It serves as a guideline for students, staff and even parents, promoting the use of language that supports emotional and social wellbeing while discouraging harmful or inappropriate language.

Schools are not responsible for the language pupils bring into the classroom from their homes. As children get older, the language they use will be increasingly influenced by their peers and by TV, film, music and social media. It is inevitable that use of inappropriate language will be an issue for most teachers in their classrooms at some stage, regardless of the age of the children or the level of intent.

A language charter can help keep students safe by setting clear boundaries on what is acceptable and unacceptable in terms of verbal interactions. For example, it can address issues such as name-calling, teasing and the use of derogatory or offensive terms. By establishing a common understanding of respectful communication, a language charter empowers students to hold themselves and others accountable for their language choices.

The implementation of a language charter also encourages early intervention when harmful or inappropriate language is used. Teachers and staff can use the charter as a reference point when addressing such language, providing a consistent framework for discussing why certain words or phrases are hurtful. This proactive approach helps prevent bullying and verbal abuse, ensuring that the school remains a safe and supportive environment for all students.

Where language charters have been implemented successfully in schools, they are used as a precursor to disciplinary action. Restorative conversations are had about the language that has been used and the impact on the person or group affected by the language, and an agreement is reached over future use of language. Parents and students appreciate this common-sense approach to behaviour that is often a result of naïvety, ignorance or poor judgement as opposed to anything more sinister.

LANGUAGE AND INCLUSION

In the safety of a school setting, language has the power to either create barriers or build bridges. It plays a fundamental role in fostering a sense of belonging and inclusion among children from diverse backgrounds. The language that teachers and students choose to use, both consciously and unconsciously, formally and informally, can either promote inclusion and mutual respect or perpetuate feelings of isolation and exclusion. Ensuring that language is inclusive is a critical element of supporting every pupil's wellbeing, helping them to feel valued, respected and understood, regardless of their personal or cultural identity.

For students from minority groups, whether due to race, gender or learning differences, inclusive language can be incredibly empowering. It reassures students that they belong, that their experiences are valid and that their voices matter. This kind of environment not only boosts individual self-esteem but also contributes to a more positive and supportive school culture where diversity is celebrated, and all students have the opportunity to flourish in the safety afforded to them by this culture.

When students feel that their identities are respected and that they are seen and valued for who they are, their overall wellbeing improves. Inclusive language fosters a sense of safety and belonging, critical for emotional and social development. A classroom that actively promotes inclusive language helps students to thrive by encouraging them to be themselves without fear of being marginalised.

ASIDE

Five strategies for using language to support wellbeing in the classroom

1. **Positive language:** Teachers should use positive and encouraging language consistently with students. When giving feedback or managing behaviour, use language that promotes growth, resilience and confidence. For example, instead of saying, 'This isn't right', try saying 'I'm interested in how you arrived at this answer', before supporting them and putting them back on the right path.
2. **Promote emotional expression:** Create opportunities for students to express their feelings through language and conversation. Regular check-ins or feelings-based discussions can help students feel more comfortable expressing their emotions. Provide sentence starters that reframe the conversation, such as 'I feel ...' or 'I am upset because ...' to help students practise expressive language and promote responsibility.
3. **Develop a language charter:** Use a language charter that sets clear guidelines for respectful communication at school. This helps prevent harmful language from undermining your behaviour policies and school values. Promote positive interactions and create a common understanding of which language is appropriate. Involve students, parents and teachers in creating the charter to ensure buy-in and commitment.
4. **Address harmful language immediately:** When inappropriate language is used, address it immediately in a calm and matter-of-fact manner. Explain why the language is problematic. And, if appropriate, offer alternative, more respectful words or phrases. This helps create a teaching moment and reinforces the importance of positive language in the classroom.
5. **Celebrate inclusive language:** Highlight and celebrate the respectful and inclusive use of language. Applaud students for using language to uplift, celebrate and motivate others, and incorporate discussions about diversity, respect and empathy into the curriculum.

MEANING

Meaning plays a vital role in a child's overall wellbeing, but can often be quite a tricky concept to explain and integrate practically into the classroom.

The very notion of what life 'means' or what meaning there is to be derived from life can present problems to adult minds if challenged with these ideas, let alone the minds of children. Within the PERMA (Positive emotions, Engagement, Relationships, Meaning, Accomplishment) framework, 'meaning' simply refers to having a sense of purpose and feeling connected to something larger than oneself. For children, this could be as basic as feeling part of a classroom community or understanding how their actions contribute to a larger purpose or goal. As children become teens and young adults, meaning starts to become connected with their aims and aspirations, career choices or what they want to achieve in life.

A child's aims will vary depending on their family background, socio-economic status, and skills, talents and academic performance. While we want children to succeed and achieve in order to live a fulfilling and meaningful life, it is important that our own preconceptions of what success looks like for a person should not prejudice how we support a person in finding their own path in life.

For some, having a family, a loving and caring partner and children of their own may be as ambitious as they dare to dream, particularly if they are from a dysfunctional family, an abusive home or were born into poverty or neglect. For others, their religion or cultural expectations may influence what they deem as being meaningful in life. Respecting diversity in this area is crucial.

As adults, it can be difficult to appreciate the ways in which children's career ambitions have shifted in recent decades. Twenty or thirty years ago, children aspired to be doctors, lawyers, nurses, police and fire people, whereas now, many children hope to become YouTubers, gamers, influencers and content creators, as the people in these roles occupy influential positions in their own lives and act as the role models of today. Though it is easy for adults to be dismissive of these aspirations, there are hundreds of thousands of young people making a living in these fields, and that is only set to increase in the future.

WHY MEANING MATTERS TO WELLBEING

Beyond career aspirations and thoughts of what adult life may look like, children thrive when they feel that what they are learning or doing has purpose beyond the classroom. By fostering a sense of meaning, teachers help students experience fulfilment, not just from academic achievements but from understanding how their efforts contribute to a larger picture; whether that involves helping others, participating in a group or understanding how knowledge connects the learning to real-world issues.

For example, when children see how a small act of kindness contributes to a positive classroom atmosphere, or when they engage in community service, they are given a clear sense of how their actions matter. These moments of contribution build a foundation for lifelong wellbeing and help produce adults who will be positive contributors to their communities.

A strong sense of meaning can buffer children against stress and anxiety, giving them a source of resilience during challenging times. The disengaged child can find themselves more motivated to devote time and energy to a task that connects them to the world outside of the classroom. Most English teachers have no doubt lost count of the number of times a student has asked 'Why are we studying *Romeo and Juliet*? How is this going to help me become an electrician?'.

Even though there is a well-rehearsed and reasonable response to this common frustration with Shakespeare that English teachers roll out on such occasions, you can't help but understand why a young person might ask this question when they are trying to find meaning in the task.

The responsibility lies with the teacher, and anyone passionate about their subject will know instinctively how the skill or knowledge being taught will impact the lives of the students. However, the process of making it explicit can often be overlooked. When I worked in an inner-city school in Nottingham, my small group of bottom-set English boys were intrigued by the gang mentality of Mercutio and how this drove the hatred between the Montagues and Capulets. The issue of off-limits romance also got their attention and with these links to their own lives and experiences established, the task became meaningful and Shakespeare stopped being the drag it had previously been.

Crucially, *meaning* acts as a stabiliser for emotional wellbeing. During periods of difficulty and struggle – such as failure, disappointment or social conflict – children with a strong sense of meaning can draw on their purpose as a source of strength. For example, if a pupil is struggling academically, knowing that their effort contributes to future goals, or that the learning helps them make a difference to someone or something, can provide the motivation to persist. Similarly, understanding how small acts of kindness or teamwork contribute to the wellbeing of others fosters a sense of social responsibility and empathy that make the behaviour worthwhile.

The teacher plays a key role in grounding the pupil and redirecting them back to this sense of meaning when their resilience is low, reminding them that temporary struggle or failure must not detract them from their wider, longer-term goals.

ASIDE

1. **Connect learning to real-world problems.** Pupils are more likely to find meaning in their learning when they see how what they learn applies to the world around them. For example, a lesson about environmental sustainability can be paired with a discussion about climate change or a school project that includes an initiative to recycle. Science classes can emphasise practical applications when learning about ecosystems, adding in challenges for older students to find solutions to present-day problems. Meanwhile, history lessons can highlight the importance of understanding past events in order to shape a better future. Create a class project where students work in groups to research solutions to real-world problems, such as plastic pollution or endangered species. These projects give students the opportunity to see how their knowledge can impact the world outside the classroom and prepare them for life beyond education.

2. **Encourage students to reflect on their own values.** Reflection is a powerful tool for creating meaning. Give students an opportunity to identify their values, interests and goals, encouraging them to consider how their actions inside and outside of the classroom align with those values. This reflective process helps children understand how their behaviour and choices contribute to a larger purpose. Use a simple note-taking exercise where students reflect on what is important to them. 'What was the most meaningful thing I did today?' or 'How did I help someone today?'. Such prompts help guide students to recognise the importance and impact of their actions.

3. **Provide opportunities for participation.** A sense of meaning often comes from feeling useful and necessary. Create opportunities for pupils to make a meaningful contribution to the classroom environment. Assign roles and responsibilities that give them ownership of different aspects of life in the classroom, such as leading discussions, organising group activities or helping younger students with small tasks. Introduce a 'classroom buddy' system

where students take on various roles, such as classroom representatives, reading mentors or leaders in sustainability. These roles give students the opportunity to participate in explicit ways and see the positive impact of their actions. Use their character strengths when assigning roles so they thrive in the roles they are given.

4. **Involve students in community projects.** Connecting children with the wider community helps them find meaning beyond their surroundings. Participation in community-service projects, whether within the school or in the local community, helps students feel a sense of belonging to something bigger than themselves. Organise a class project where students volunteer for a local charity or lead a charity fundraiser to create that sense of purpose. Planting trees or cleaning up the local park or beach allows children to connect with their environment and feel a sense of pride in their accomplishments. This also helps students see the direct impact of their efforts and promotes a sense of social responsibility.

5. **Highlight the role of meaning in success stories.** Show students examples of people who became successful by doing meaningful things. Whether through books, films or guest speakers, highlight the role of meaning in their journey. Discuss how each person's sense of purpose contributed to their success and personal growth. These stories should be inspiring and show how meaning drives fulfilment. Use history lessons to look at figures from the past who have been influential in our lives today, or take a more modern look by asking children to make a short presentation about an influencer they admire who overcame challenges by connecting with their purpose. Have students discuss or write about what drives these individuals and how they might apply the things they have learned to their own lives.

NURTURING

Our children inhabit a world where gratification is expected and demanded at a speed most adults are unable to understand. Mastery of a video game can be achieved by paying money to increase or improve the character strengths or variables needed in the game to succeed. Social-media algorithms ensure young people have precisely the type of media content they need at a given time; they barely have to search for it. Access to friends, wherever they may be around the world, can be organised at the touch of a button.

The internet and AI are eroding the need to build up knowledge in a particular subject area when it can be easily found/recalled within seconds. If you ever need proof of this, try to sit and watch a full-length film with a class of teenagers, or suggest doing a jigsaw or playing a game of Monopoly with any children in your family. See what response you get after ten minutes or so; 'boring!'. The shortcuts that are available through digital technology have led to a reduced resilience and attention span in some children and young people, yet these skills are essential for development and preparation for adulthood. Resilience is the ability to bounce back from setbacks, to persist in the face of difficulty and to maintain a positive outlook even when things don't go as planned.

Nurturing students' resilience is crucial for enabling them to overcome academic challenges, navigate social pressures and manage their emotional wellbeing.

Carol Dweck's concept of a 'growth mindset' (2016) is closely aligned with resilience. Dweck's research suggests that when students believe their abilities can grow with effort and persistence, they are more likely to face challenges with a positive attitude. Her work is essential reading if this is a concept that you wish to explore further.

Students with a growth mindset understand that failure is not a permanent state but rather a stepping stone to improvement. This mindset encourages resilience because it shifts the focus from fear of failure to the importance of learning and growing from experiences. On the flip side, a child who is not resilient will quickly become disengaged, disillusioned and see failure as final and, therefore, damaging. The child who lacks resilience can become risk-averse in their learning and avoid challenges. This, in turn, can lead to fear and anxiety, neither of which are conducive to positive wellbeing.

A resilient-focused classroom pays greater attention to the learning *journey* rather than the destination, result or grade. The end result and how it was achieved should be celebrated equally. This requires reflection and giving the students the opportunity to think about the following:

1. What they knew before the task/lesson/project.
2. What skills they needed to employ.
3. Where and why the learning got difficult.
4. What action they took to overcome the difficulty.
5. How they felt when they completed the task/lesson/project.

The work of James Nottingham (2017) visualises this as a 'learning pit' whereby students go through a range of experiences and emotions before being able to climb out of 'the pit'. Notice from the diagram how they emerge from the pit into new ground, slightly more elevated than their starting point, showing growth and development. In some classes, this diagram is displayed as a poster in a prominent position in the classroom. When students approach the teacher for help, they are asked to show on the diagram where they are in the 'pit' and what stage of learning they are at. The teacher then asks questions about how the students can use pre-taught pathways and strategies to help themselves out of this pit. These can be as simple as:

1. Go back and try something different.
2. Re-read the material/the task.

3. Consult a friend.
4. Come back with more specific questions. ('I don't get it' and 'Can you help me?' were not allowed in the class I observed.)
5. Make a list of the parts of the task you do understand and the parts you don't to identify the specific area in which you need support.

James Nottingham's 'learning pit'

RESILIENCE: A LIFELONG SKILL

Teachers and leaders need to nurture resilience. Resilience not only helps students succeed in the classroom but also equips them with essential life skills. By learning how to bounce back from setbacks, students develop the emotional strength and flexibility needed to navigate life's inevitable challenges. In addition, resilience contributes to better mental health, as it reduces the impact of stress and anxiety and helps students maintain a positive outlook.

By integrating resilience-building strategies into everyday classroom activities, teachers can create an environment where students feel empowered to face challenges, learn from failures and grow as individuals. When students understand that setbacks are temporary and manageable, they are more likely to persevere through difficulties, both academically and personally.

Nurturing resilience in students is about much more than just helping them succeed academically. It's about teaching them how to navigate the ups and downs of life with confidence, adaptability and perseverance. By fostering a growth mindset, normalising setbacks, encouraging problem-solving and providing emotional support, teachers can help students develop the resilience they need to thrive in school and beyond.

RESILIENCE: BUILDING EMOTIONAL STRENGTH

The process of building resilience in young people is not easy. It involves encouraging a sense of responsibility, perseverance and self-awareness from a very early age. A child's resilience also depends to a large extent on how they are treated at home. A home life where everything is done on behalf of the child and made easy for them does not promote resilience. Therefore, teachers play a critical role in modelling resilience and providing students with the tools they need to face challenges constructively. It's important to remember that resilience can be learned, and the classroom offers countless opportunities for students to practise and develop this essential life skill.

ASIDE

Nurturing resilience

1. **Promote a growth mindset:** Encourage effort over results and celebrate progress, not just achievement. How are pupils rewarded in your class and in your school? If it is for grades/scores only, this alienates those pupils who may never be able to attain the grades that (potentially) come easy/without too much effort for others. They will quickly realise they are in a no-win situation and that willingness to put in effort will, over time, be eroded.

2. **Normalise mistakes:** Create a classroom culture where mistakes are viewed as learning opportunities. The ground rules in the classroom should be clearly established from day one whether that relates to hands up/hands down questioning, thinking time or how the class supports and assists another learner when a mistake is made. Instil the mantra 'I can't do it … yet' as a reminder that growth follows a challenge.

3. **Encourage problem-solving:** Guide students to think critically and independently when facing challenges. Provide them with a clear pathway of ways to solve a problem independently, or by using peers, before they ask a teacher to intervene. Over-reliance on teachers does not build resilience.

4. **Build supportive relationships:** Foster a sense of belonging and trust through positive teacher–student interactions. If a student feels that you believe in them, and you have the relationship in place to keep pushing them further than they thought they could go, they will achieve more.

5. **Teach emotional regulation:** Incorporate mindfulness activities when the going gets tough and children are on the verge of the 'giving up' moment. Help them to ground and centre using breathing exercises and other tools to enable them to manage stress, refocus and re-engage.

OPENNESS

Wellbeing cannot flourish in an environment where it is not part of the culture to speak openly and honestly about feelings.

The stigma around mental health exists because of a lack of understanding which, in itself, is a result of mental health not being spoken openly about by the previous generations. In fact, the word 'stigma' can be traced back to ancient Greek and means to 'carve or mark as a sign of shame, punishment or disgrace'. For thousands of years, persons suffering from mental health issues were treated no better than criminals and slaves, who themselves were branded in order to identify them as being sub-human.

A superb therapeutic practitioner who talks with authority on this topic asks this question to his audience when he talks on the topic: 'Who has mental health?'. Regardless of whether there are adults, professionals, children or teens present, the response is indicative of the connotations that still exist around the term. One or two hands slowly go up. Most look around nervously to see what the rest of the audience is doing. Some busy themselves with checking the time on their phone or readjusting their ties.

The correct answer, of course, is that we *all* have mental health and we *all* have wellbeing. In most classrooms, especially in infant and junior schools, conversations about feelings and emotions take place quite organically as children speak much more openly and naturally about what they are experiencing when they are young. As children enter their teen years, and their feelings and emotions become more intense and confusing, talking about emotional or physical growth/change can be 'cringe' or be met with ridicule and embarrassment by their peers. Those of you who have delivered RSE (personal, social, health (and economic) education) lessons in your career will recall the snorts of embarrassment and sharp intakes of breath at the first mention of the word 'puberty', for example.

While it might feel like a gargantuan task to arm the pupils in our schools with the language they need to be more open, research has shown that it can be achieved in as little as 10 minutes a day. There are free programmes available on the internet around emotional intelligence that provide teachers and students with the tools and language they need to be able to communicate more effectively. Character strengths and the six virtues (see the chapter 'Character') are also a perfect starting point and allow pupils to apply that new knowledge and language to themselves and others before more complex and abstract concepts are introduced as they become more confident.

TOO OPEN?

Finding a balance around openness and understanding of wellbeing and mental health is crucial. As children become more familiar and comfortable with wellbeing and mental health language, it can sometimes be adopted as a tool to self-diagnose (misdiagnose?) regular emotions and experiences. The following are all examples of classic self/misdiagnoses teachers regularly encounter in their classrooms:

- A pupil who was worried about a test claimed that he had an anxiety disorder. He didn't – the teacher checked – he was simply feeling *nervous*.
- A teen who had just split from her boyfriend said she was clinically depressed. She wasn't – the teacher checked – she was feeling *sad*.
- A student who wasn't able to focus on some complex theory that was being taught told the teacher he thought he had ADHD (attention deficit hyperactivity disorder). He didn't – the teacher checked – he was struggling to *focus*.
- A girl who was overheard telling her friend, as she fussed around organising all her pens in height and colour order, that she had OCD (obsessive-compulsive disorder). She didn't – she just wanted

to maintain a tidy pencil case as a distraction from the maths work she was supposed to be doing.

These children were using language about mental health conditions to describe temporary feelings. Adults can be as guilty of this as children.

On the one hand, we want to congratulate these students for talking openly about their feelings because all of them were valid. No matter how important or petty some of them may sound, there was enough thinking and reflection going on in the students' minds to verbalise and articulate how something made them *feel*.

On the other hand, trivialising such conditions and self-diagnosing can serve to reduce the actual condition to a quirk, or even something quite cute, when the truth is that anxiety, depression, ADHD and OCD can be debilitating and, at their extremes, destroy lives. Let's not be too harsh on children misusing these terms, though. Like any new language, concept or idea, trying it out, playing around with it and getting it wrong are all part of the process that will ultimately result in them getting it right. They just need guidance.

A simple activity that helps students navigate states of wellbeing (flourishing and languishing) and how they intersect with mental health (diagnosis of a mental health condition through to no diagnosed mental health condition) is to talk through the mental health continuum model. This helps students visualise the notion that a person can have a mental health condition and still experience positive wellbeing, but also that even if a person's wellbeing is very low/poor, it does not necessarily mean that they have a mental health condition. It is useful to discuss with your class what it might look and feel like to be in one of the four quadrants of the graph.

THE A–Z OF STUDENT WELLBEING

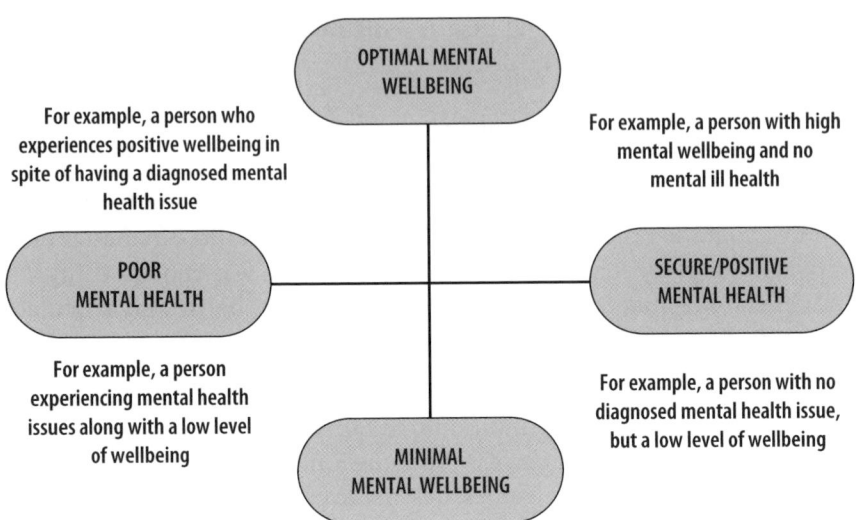

The relationship between wellbeing and mental ill health

FINDING THE BALANCE

It can be overwhelming and quite frightening to teach only the language and conditions that relate to illbeing and mental health conditions. A more balanced approach is to consider wellbeing and mental health as a continuum, whereby flourishing, happiness, character strengths and thriving are given an equal amount of airtime in the classroom as anxiety, depression, eating disorders, self-harm and suicide.

A classroom and school that has access to this breadth of understanding about wellbeing and mental health is better equipped to be more open and accepting around *all* states of wellbeing. Children who don't have access to this language will either grow up misunderstanding wellbeing and mental health concepts – misusing the terminology, incorrectly self-diagnosing – or avoid discussions on the topic altogether.

OPENNESS

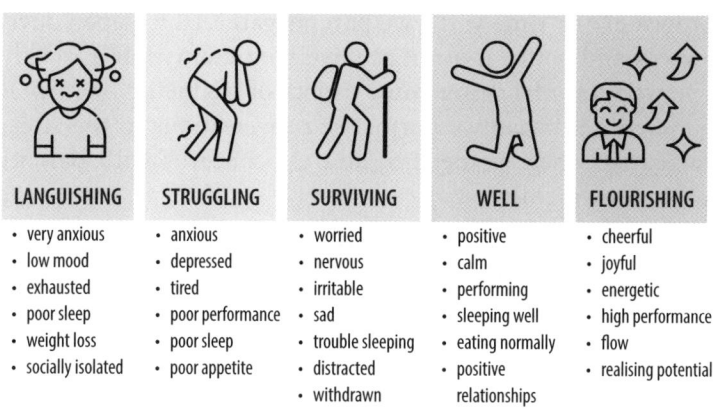

LANGUISHING	STRUGGLING	SURVIVING	WELL	FLOURISHING
• very anxious • low mood • exhausted • poor sleep • weight loss • socially isolated	• anxious • depressed • tired • poor performance • poor sleep • poor appetite	• worried • nervous • irritable • sad • trouble sleeping • distracted • withdrawn	• positive • calm • performing • sleeping well • eating normally • positive relationships	• cheerful • joyful • energetic • high performance • flow • realising potential

The mental health continuum model
Adapted from Al Taher, 2016, Character Strengths and Virtues: The Classification Explained

A WHOLE-SCHOOL APPROACH

An open and honest approach to wellbeing in a school can only be achieved in a culture that is purposely designed to welcome and promote such openness and inclusivity. Be aware of the power of the staffroom sceptics who can undermine a school's efforts to promote wellbeing. In the minds of some, there is still a belief that it is a teacher's job to teach the academics and that pastoral responsibilities are someone else's business. Thankfully, such dissenting voices are now in the minority as the role of the teacher has changed considerably in the last 20–30 years. Likewise, there may be opposition to an open and honest culture in your school from your parents.

In some cultures, there may be resistance when a child is referred to the school counsellor, for example. Many adults still equate counselling with mental 'illness' or, worse, mental 'weakness' and having their child put on the 'therapist's couch' and be made to divulge all the horrors from their childhood will be the stereotype some have taken from film and TV.

Be honest from the moment a family joins your school. Outline your approach to wellbeing and mental health in your literature and prospectus from the outset. Have counsellors and pastoral leads speak about your provision any time you have parents gathered for open days, curriculum events and coffee mornings. Give your counsellor a weekly spot in your newsletter, or feature some aspect of wellbeing or mental health on your website. When we normalise conversations in this area, it makes it far easier when we need to address concerns with parents directly about their own child.

As difficult as it can be, enable your community to have access to the facts. In the last NHS report on the state of mental health in young people (NHS, 2023) it was reported that 1 in 5 young people (aged 8–25) have a mental health condition. For many parents, this may come as a shockingly high statistic, but in the event their child does develop a condition or struggle with their wellbeing, being forewarned is being forearmed. Parents need guiding through the difficulties their children will face and schools are increasingly becoming the frontline for such support in the community.

With services such as CAMHS (Child and Adolescent Mental Health Services) and the NHS experiencing cuts in their funding, we now find ourselves playing an important role in supporting the wellbeing and mental health of our young people. It is no longer 'someone else's job'; it is very much ours.

ASIDE

Being open

1. **Communicate regularly about wellbeing and mental health.** Share with your parents the work and progress undertaken in each classroom so they are part of the journey their children are on.

2. **Take the opportunity to outline your whole-school approach to wellbeing and mental health whenever you have an audience.** Constant reinforcement of your school's ethos and commitment to wellbeing serves to normalise some of the language and concepts that you value.

3. **Give a voice and a platform to your pastoral leads and your counsellors.** These people should be visible and accessible. Be transparent about the work they do, their purpose and their role. For some parents, these positions would not have existed back when they were at school.

4. **Introduce new language and new concepts around wellbeing and mental health at the appropriate ages.** Ensure your school has a plan from the earliest year you take children in, until the oldest year. Spiral that plan upwards so basic terminology is introduced, embedded and added to year on year so that it becomes increasingly more sophisticated.

5. **Normalise conversations about emotions.** Be conscious of the fact that students can go from being very open to sometimes very closed within a matter of months as adolescence hits. Keep lines of communication open and don't allow silence to breed a culture of fear or mistrust when it comes to wellbeing and mental health.

PERMA

AN INTRODUCTION TO PERMA

Whenever we speak about or teach aspects of PERMA, we should be advised to do so with the warning that PERMA is not a magical wellbeing secret that will revolutionise the way we think about what it means to be happy or well. In fact, it is little more than a framework of common sense already proven by thousands of years of assumed knowledge that has been rubber-stamped by science in more recent times.

PERMA is a foundational model in positive psychology developed by Dr Martin Seligman, and it stands for Positive emotions, Engagement, Relationships, Meaning and Accomplishment. Some models have been updated in recent years to include a letter 'H' at the end to represent physical health. This framework offers a comprehensive approach to understanding and fostering wellbeing, not only in individual lives but also within educational environments and beyond.

When applied in schools, PERMA provides a structure that supports students' overall wellbeing, gives pastoral teams and leaders an evidence-based theoretical starting point, and encourages positive mental health. In essence, PERMA gives you a name for the things that make life meaningful, but makes them more explicit, specific and accessible.

The model relies on a cycle of engagement from all stakeholders using the following mantra: 'learn it, live it, teach it, embed it'. This can be problematic for some teachers who may not feel it necessary to have to 'live' and experience something in their own lives that is being taught by them in their classrooms or demanded of them in their schools. But why wouldn't we all want to thrive in these areas of wellbeing? What reasons would anyone have not to want to experience and flourish in all of these areas? The teacher who has the wellbeing of their students at heart, has these five areas of wellbeing firmly in mind in everything they plan and deliver in the classroom. Let's take a look at each one in more depth.

POSITIVE EMOTIONS

A healthy school should be awash with these throughout the day. The best schools are joyful ones, where that joy runs like a seam through play, teaching and learning, relationships and staff wellbeing. Positive emotions such as joy, gratitude and hope are crucial for students' wellbeing. These emotions enhance learning, improve problem-solving abilities and foster a more inclusive and empathetic classroom atmosphere. Positive emotions also contribute to a student's resilience, helping them cope better with challenges.

In our schools, it should be relatively straightforward for us to be able to foster positive emotions that can be achieved through practices like the gratitude exercises (discussed earlier in the chapter 'Gratitude'), celebrations of achievements, and creating moments of joy, such as interactive learning games or recognition of effort, character strengths, manners and kindness, no matter how small the gesture. When students feel good emotionally, they are more open to learning and engaging with others. This is as important for students in the sixth form as it is for those in early years. Though the manner in which these emotions are engaged will differ according to age, they are still crucial to wellbeing.

ENGAGEMENT

The inclusion of engagement within the PERMA model serves to reinforce just how important it is to wellbeing and learning that the classroom is a place where students are engaged. Engagement refers to a deep involvement in activities that challenge us and absorb our attention. When students are truly engaged, they experience 'flow'. In this state, students are so immersed in what they are doing that time seems to fly. Engagement is linked to motivation and perseverance, both of which are key to achieving academic and personal goals. Quite often, it is through the acknowledgement of what engages a student that they first start to connect with ambitions beyond school: careers, jobs or further education.

For teachers, encouraging engagement means creating learning experiences that are both stimulating and accessible. This can include hands-on projects, collaborative group work or problem-solving activities that relate to real-world issues. Tailoring tasks to individual student strengths can also heighten their interest and investment in learning.

RELATIONSHIPS

Positive relationships are fundamental to wellbeing, particularly in school settings where peer interaction is central to students' lives. Having healthy friendships and feeling connected to teachers and other adults within the school fosters a sense of belonging and safety. Schools can encourage positive relationships by promoting teamwork, peer mentoring and respectful communication. Teachers play a crucial role in modelling positive social interactions, ensuring that students feel heard and valued. Creating an inclusive environment where students can form meaningful relationships can lead to a more supportive and cohesive school community.

MEANING

This aspect of PERMA is perhaps the most difficult one for teachers to get to grips with and make practical application of in their classrooms. Meaning relates to having a sense of purpose and understanding how one's actions contribute to something greater than oneself. For students, finding meaning in what they learn or how they contribute to the school environment can enhance their overall sense of fulfilment. 'Meaning' can sometimes feel too grandiose a term to use successfully in a classroom setting, but it can be achieved without delving too far into the realms of existentialism.

To foster meaning in the classroom, teachers can link lessons to broader societal issues, encourage students to reflect on the impact of their actions and create opportunities for community involvement. Whether through service learning, environmental projects or exploring career aspirations, when students see that their work has purpose, they are more motivated and engaged. Students that can see an output, an end-goal or an aim, be it inside or outside of the classroom, are more likely to engage as a result of the activity or task having meaning.

ACCOMPLISHMENT

Whenever I think about the importance of accomplishment in PERMA and to a child's wellbeing, I can't help but think back to my own school days. I was very small for my age, so I was always the last to be picked at football, was barely noticed in PE or at sports days, and never played for a school team. Academically, I coasted to average grades in class and failed at every musical instrument I ever picked up. If the story ended there, you would assume I had a pretty awful time at school, but I didn't. For the most part, I enjoyed school.

I particularly enjoyed it when I was in the company of one of those inspirational teachers who just made you feel special, regardless of whether you were top of the class or bottom. The magic they had was the ability to make you feel like you'd 'accomplished' something, no matter how big or small. At infant or junior school, that was as simple as recognising learning milestones as they were achieved. At senior school, my drama teacher recognised some acting talent within me and helped me get into a few local films and theatre groups, giving me not only a sense of accomplishment but also a sense of meaning for my life at that time.

It is because of those few teachers that I am a teacher myself today. It can often be understated how impactful we are in this very special position of influence that we occupy, but lives truly are shaped by teachers and I am sure you all have a very similar tale of your own to tell. Think back to what role that inspirational teacher played in your life; how they made you feel accomplished in some shape or form.

Accomplishment refers to the sense of achievement that comes from setting and reaching goals. In school, accomplishments can range from mastering a challenging concept to completing a long-term project or developing a new skill. Acknowledging student achievement is vital for building self-esteem and resilience. Schools can create an environment of accomplishment by setting clear goals, providing constructive feedback and celebrating successes through awards, certificates or simple acknowledgments.

By celebrating growth and effort over perfection, children learn to value the learning process itself, building a lifelong love of learning in the process.

ASIDE

Why PERMA matters for wellbeing in schools

- **Improving academic performance.** When students experience a wide range of positive emotions, their academic performance improves and they are more likely to participate and engage.
- **Supporting mental health.** PERMA promotes a holistic approach to mental health, focusing on the positive aspects of wellbeing rather than addressing issues such as anxiety or depression. This does not require teachers to receive expert mental health training or possess advanced knowledge. By giving students the tools to build resilience and maintain a positive attitude, schools can better support their emotional intelligence.
- **Promoting a positive school culture.** Schools that adopt the PERMA model are more likely to have a positive culture where staff and students feel valued. This culture of respect, understanding and support creates a safer and more productive learning environment. For example, schools in the UAE adopted PERMA as a nationwide initiative in schools to improve wellbeing.
- **Promoting lifelong health.** PERMA principles don't just apply in schools. They serve as tools that students can use into adulthood and include learning how to promote positive emotions, engaging with the world, building strong relationships, being more aware of meaning and celebrating success. These all help students to develop a foundation for lifelong wellbeing.

To consider:

1. What does your curriculum and overall school experience look like when viewed through the lens of PERMA?
2. Cast your mind back to your last full day of teaching. Where were the 'PERMA moments' for your students? How can you create opportunities for more in each of the five areas?
3. If you are introducing PERMA for the first time, see whether your students can guess what the five concepts are for a fulfilling life. It will be interesting to compare what is important to them to the science.
4. What does PERMA look like in your own life? Is there a balance in each of the five areas or is your job creating an unhealthy balance somewhere? How can this be addressed?
5. PERMA and character strengths are a powerful combination. Challenge students to identify the links between the two.

QUESTIONING

Questions are more than just a tool for gathering information and checking understanding; they are the first (and, perhaps, most basic) tool for exploration, reflection and growth. In class, the types of questions teachers ask, and the way they are framed, can have a profound impact on a pupil's wellbeing. A skilled teacher can get to the heart of the matter with only a handful of carefully chosen, pertinent questions.

Thoughtful, open-ended questioning not only engages students in learning but also fosters a sense of curiosity, self-awareness and emotional intelligence. When students are encouraged to ask questions themselves, reflect on their own learning or wellbeing, and feel that their voices are heard, their sense of self-worth, autonomy and belonging is strengthened.

For a child's wellbeing to thrive, they need to feel safe to express their thoughts and explore their ideas without fear of judgement. Through careful questioning, teachers can create an environment that supports both intellectual development and emotional wellbeing. Asking questions that challenge students to think critically, reflect on their experiences, and explore their emotions fosters a growth mindset, helping them navigate challenges with resilience and confidence.

WHY QUESTIONING MATTERS FOR WELLBEING

When we are talking to a child about any aspect of their wellbeing or mental health, we are potentially encroaching on personal and sensitive matters which the child could perceive as a threat. The wording of questions, and the tone in which they are asked, will directly impact on how safe the child feels in responding openly and honestly. Consider the question 'What is wrong with you?' asked by the teacher who is naïve or ignorant about how questions should be carefully worded.

First of all, the assumption that whatever the child is experiencing is 'wrong' already raises a red flag about how this will be perceived. The direct question also puts the onus onto the child, relying on them having the emotional intelligence, skills and vocabulary to articulate how they are feeling in response. The pressure created by this question perhaps stems from the need for the teacher to obtain a quick resolution to the issue and, in this haste, positive wellbeing solutions for the child cannot be achieved.

'What's wrong with you?'

'Billy won't play with me.'

'Well go and find someone else to play with then.'

Questioning should serve as a powerful tool to enable emotional expression. Questions that encourage children to articulate their feelings, such as, 'How did this make you feel?' or 'What did you learn about yourself in this situation?', help children process their emotions. Additionally, asking students to consider the feelings of others promotes empathy, a key component of social and emotional wellbeing. This practice helps students develop healthier relationships and a greater understanding of the perspectives and emotions of those around them.

'Why won't Billy play with me?'

'Why don't we go and find somewhere quiet so we can talk about this in more detail?'

When students feel their questions are valued and taken seriously, their confidence grows. This sense of autonomy, the belief that they have control over their learning and thoughts, is essential for building resilience. By framing questions in a way that encourages students to see challenges as opportunities for growth, teachers nurture resilience and foster a mindset that values learning and problem-solving.

'Have you asked Billy why he doesn't want to play with you?'

'If Billy was here now, what might he say if we asked him together why he doesn't want to play with you?'

'If Billy doesn't want to play with you, what are some other options for playtime?'

The types of questions can set the tone for the entire school environment. Open-ended, non-judgmental questions foster a sense of psychological safety, where students feel comfortable expressing their ideas without fear of being wrong or judged. The questions being asked are not apportioning blame or creating any shame around why Billy might not want to play with this child. Instead, this inclusive approach helps all students, including those who may be quieter or less confident, to participate and feel valued and heard.

Schools where questions are used to encourage exploration, rather than simply find out facts and resolve issues, are schools where the students learn to take more responsibility for their actions.

QUESTIONING FOR WELLBEING, NOT JUST FOR LEARNING

An effective teacher already understands the importance of questioning for learning; it is an essential tool. The effective wellbeing practitioner uses questioning in exactly the same way, challenging children to engage at a deeper level with the situation or emotion before them. When questions are used to shame, belittle or create fear, such as 'What is your mum going to say when I tell her about this?' or 'Are you proud of yourself?', the child's wellbeing is adversely affected and questions are used as a threat and a criticism.

There is no room for a child's voice to be heard when questioning is used aggressively, and it creates a vacuum, leaving no space for restorative practice or social/emotional learning to take place. Sadly, too many teachers still use questions to put words in the mouths of pupils in order for them to experience shame, in the faint hope that this feeling discourages them from acting that way again: 'So you completely ignored what I said and did what you wanted anyway, did you?'. We would never use questioning in a learning context in such a way, yet for some reason, one of our most effective tools becomes blunted when we change the focus from learning to wellbeing.

ASIDE

1. **Use open-ended questions.** Open-ended questions, such as 'How are you feeling about this task?' or 'What would you like to happen next?' provide students with the space to share their thoughts, emotions and concerns. These questions promote reflection and deeper conversation, allowing teachers to gain insights into the student's emotional and mental state. Closed questions are effective where a student is completely unable or unwilling to respond verbally and facts need to be established quickly and efficiently.

2. **Frame questions with empathy.** Ensure your questions are phrased in a way that shows understanding and support. For example, instead of asking 'Why didn't you do the homework?', consider asking, 'What challenges did you face with this task?'. This shows the student that you are there to help, rather than to judge. One question can be seen as a threat, the other as supportive.

3. **Incorporate regular emotional check-ins.** Make emotional check-ins a routine part of your classroom practice. Questions like 'How are you feeling today?' or 'What's something that made you feel proud this week?' help normalise conversations about emotions and provide a safe space for students to express themselves. Ensuring a balance exists between questions about the learning and questions about the learner shows your interest in both.

4. **Ask reflective questions to promote self-esteem.** Encourage students to reflect on their learning process and how they can grow from challenges. Questions such as 'What did you learn from that?' or 'How might you approach this differently next time?' build resilience and help students see challenges as a normal part of the learning process.

5. **Encourage peer-to-peer questioning for empathy.** Model and encourage students to ask supportive questions to one another. Questions like 'How do you think your classmate might have felt during that situation?' promote empathy, understanding and a sense of community within the classroom. Asking students to reposition themselves as others who they may have impacted, either negatively or positively, forces them to consider the impact of their actions without directly causing or implying shame.

RESTORATIVE

Restorative practices are an essential approach to fostering wellbeing in schools. They focus on building, maintaining and repairing relationships, promoting a culture of accountability, respect and mutual understanding.

Restorative practices are a proactive and relational approach to addressing conflict and promoting positive behaviour, highlighting the importance of relationships, accountability and community in schools. Unlike traditional punitive measures, which focus on punishment as the primary means of correcting a behaviour, restorative practices aim to repair harm and rebuild relationships through open dialogue, empathy and mutual understanding. This method promotes emotional intelligence by encouraging students to reflect on their actions, understand their impact on others and take responsibility for making amends.

Research has shown that many schools that have adopted restorative practices have seen a decrease in school-wide misbehaviour and student mental-health challenges, as well as an improved school climate and higher levels of student achievement.

THE ROLE OF RESTORATIVE PRACTICES IN PROMOTING WELLBEING

At the heart of restorative practices is the core belief that relationships are central to learning and personal development. When students feel more connected, supported and heard, they are more likely to thrive emotionally, socially and academically. Restorative practices encourage students to participate actively in solving conflicts, understanding the impact of their actions and working towards repairing harm in a constructive manner.

Too often in our schools, conflicts are 'solved' by the teacher with the behaviour policy or rules of the school dictating what happens to the child who bullied/misbehaved. Too often, the child who was bullied or affected is not a partner in these discussions, policy becomes king and the ownership of the incident or issue is immediately devolved from the children to the adults.

A restorative approach contrasts with traditional punitive disciplinary measures, which often isolate students and fail to address the underlying causes of their behaviour. Punitive approaches can damage a student's self-esteem and sense of belonging, potentially increasing feelings of alienation or resentment.

In contrast, restorative practices aim to understand emotions, build empathy and improve connections, all of which contribute to a student's emotional wellbeing. This approach has been shown to be favoured by both the victim and the child who has caused the harm. Essentially, those who are subjected to maltreatment want to know *why* this has happened to them and want reassurances that it won't happen again. A punitive sanction can breed resentment, disconnect the child from their sense of belonging to the school and can sometimes make the situation worse, in the absence of any restorative conversation or outcome, as the children have no satisfactory resolution to their conflict aside from the punishment.

For instance, instead of being suspended for a behavioural issue, a student might participate in a restorative circle where they can talk openly about the reasons behind their actions and how they impacted others. This process encourages students to take responsibility for their behaviour while also supporting them in developing the social and emotional skills necessary to avoid similar issues in the future.

RESTORATIVE CIRCLES

Restorative circles are a key component of restorative practices. They are simply structured conversations designed to build community and resolve conflicts. Circles provide students with a safe space to share their thoughts, feelings and experiences. They are designed to promote open communication, empathy and mutual respect, which are all essential for emotional wellbeing. The voice of all students, regardless of role, is important in this process so everyone has a safe space to discuss reasons for the conflict, impact and desired outcomes.

Restorative circles can be used proactively without an instigating incident to build trust and understanding within a classroom community. For example, during regular classroom circles or talk time, students might be encouraged to share something that made them happy that week (a great opportunity to practise gratitude) or to talk about a personal goal they are working towards. These conversations help strengthen relationships among students, creating a supportive environment where everyone feels valued and heard. Students could be challenged to think of ways they can help their peers achieve their goals, forming a collective responsibility to everyone's mission to achieve and feel accomplished.

When conflicts arise, these restorative circles then provide a forum for affected individuals to come together, discuss the impact of the incident and find ways to repair harm collaboratively. This process promotes healing, reduces the likelihood of ongoing resentment and helps prevent further incidents. Importantly, it also teaches students essential life skills such as active listening, empathy and conflict resolution, all of which are critical to their social and emotional development. The teacher gets the opportunity to model effective conflict resolution and students get to engage in open, honest and constructive conversations about actions and consequences.

RESTORATIVE PRACTICE: A WHOLE SCHOOL APPROACH

For restorative practices to be truly effective, they must be embedded as part of a whole-school approach rather than being implemented in isolated instances or within individual classrooms. A whole-school approach ensures that the values and principles of restorative practices – respect, empathy, accountability and community – become an accepted part of the school culture, influencing all interactions and decision-making processes.

Restorative practice should be introduced with the aim of building and maintaining positive relationships, repairing harm, and promoting a sense of belonging and emotional safety. For these principles to resonate deeply with staff and students, they need to be consistently modelled and reinforced by all, from school leaders to classroom teachers and support staff.

When everyone in the school community is aligned with this approach, it creates a unified environment where students experience consistency in expectations, responses to behaviour, and opportunities for reflection and growth.

Furthermore, a whole-school approach allows for the early identification and resolution of conflicts before they escalate. If only certain teachers or areas of the school practice restorative methods, students may experience mixed messages about the consequences of their actions or the importance of repairing relationships. This inconsistency can undermine the effectiveness of restorative practices, as students might feel unsupported or confused about behavioural expectations.

ASIDE

Implementing restorative practices in schools requires a careful and structured process that involves commitment from the entire school community. It is a change in culture and philosophy that must be carefully introduced and nurtured to ensure success. This takes both time and money to complete. Here are some ways schools can begin this important journey.

1. The first step in implementing restorative practices is for school leaders to be fully committed to the approach and articulate a clear vision. Restorative practices represent a shift from traditional disciplinary measures to a more relationship-focused and therapeutic approach to managing behaviour and conflict.

2. Professional development for staff is essential to ensure effective implementation, and all staff must be trained in the principles and techniques of restorative practice. This includes teachers, administrative staff and support staff. Professional development should introduce key interventions of restorative practice, such as restoration circles, conflict resolution and restorative language.
3. Creating a restorative culture means embedding restorative practices into the fabric of daily school life. This requires a change in how all communities, staff, students and families interact. One effective way to start is to introduce restorative circles as a regular part of your classroom routine. Circles can be used not only to resolve conflicts, but also to build community, promote open discussion and encourage mutual respect.
4. For restorative practices to be truly effective, students need to be active participants, not passive recipients, so student voice and consultation is essential. Schools can involve students by teaching them about restorative principles before they are implemented and empowering them to take part in restorative processes as the opportunities arise.
5. Restorative practices work best when the entire school community, including families, understands and supports the approach. Schools should make efforts to engage parents and caregivers by explaining the principles of restorative practices and how they align with the school's values of respect, empathy and accountability.
6. As with any major change to whole-school policy, it is important to monitor progress and reflect on the implementation of restorative practices. Schools should regularly assess how restorative practices are being adopted and whether they are achieving the desired outcomes, such as reduced conflict, improved student behaviour and stronger relationships.

SAFEGUARDING

The entire concept of promoting the wellbeing of students is redundant in the absence of a safeguarding culture which is understood and practised by every single adult within the school environment. A robust safeguarding policy is fundamental in ensuring the safety and wellbeing of students in schools.

As a teacher or leader, you will already know that a safeguarding policy acts as a framework that schools must adhere to, providing clear guidelines on how to protect children from abuse, neglect, exploitation and harm. The importance of such a policy cannot be overstated, as it directly impacts the physical, emotional and psychological safety of students, which, in turn, influences their ability to learn and thrive.

First and foremost, a safeguarding policy establishes a protective environment within the school. It ensures that all staff, including teachers, administrators and support personnel, understand their roles and responsibilities in identifying and responding to signs of abuse or neglect. By clearly outlining procedures for reporting concerns, an effective safeguarding policy should enable swift action when a pupil's safety is at risk. This prompt response can prevent further harm and ensure that appropriate interventions are provided to support the pupil's wellbeing.

Moreover, a robust safeguarding policy helps create a culture of vigilance and accountability. When everyone in the school community is aware of the signs of potential abuse or neglect, and knows how to report them, the likelihood of incidents going unnoticed is significantly reduced. The consequences of an adult or a school missing signs of abuse, harm or neglect can be devastating and tragic.

The deaths of Victoria Climbié and Peter Connelly, known as 'Baby P' (and, to some extent, those of Holly Wells and Jessica Chapman, commonly known as the 'Soham Murders'), were tragedies that not only became shocking national headlines that highlighted unimaginable failings in the protection of children, but went on to become catalysts for the overhaul of child protection legislation that has resulted in what we refer to as 'safeguarding' today. This collective responsibility towards safeguarding creates an environment where children feel safe and supported, knowing that their concerns will be taken seriously. Such a culture also discourages potential perpetrators from attempting to harm children, as they are aware of the strong protective measures in place in terms of checking, vetting, reporting and recording of information.

TRAINING AND EDUCATION

A critical aspect of a safeguarding policy is the need for ongoing training and education. Regular training ensures that all staff members are up to date on the latest safeguarding practices and understand how to apply them effectively. This is crucial, as it equips staff with the knowledge and skills necessary to recognise the often-subtle signs of abuse, neglect or exploitation.

Depending on your school's context, location and demographics, the risks may vary and include radicalisation, FGM (female genital mutilation), gang affiliation, drug use, substance abuse, or involvement in the supply and distribution of drugs from one area to another (sometimes referred to as 'county lines'). Additionally, educating students about their rights and how to seek help if they feel unsafe is an essential component of a safeguarding policy.

Empowered children who know what safeguarding means are more likely to report abuse, contributing to a safer school environment.

If you were to ask a student in your school what 'safeguarding' means, would they be able to articulate the basic definition of the term in their own words? As teachers, we have to bear in mind that, while the concept of safeguarding is designed to protect those experiencing harm, abuse or neglect, some children may believe that the involvement of an external agency may result in greater harm being inflicted on them by their abuser. In my years of dealing with child-protection issues, the same questions and concerns are raised by the children who come to report issues, regardless of age.

> 'If I tell you something, will you promise not to tell anyone else?'
>
> 'If I tell you, it is only going to get worse.'
>
> 'It's fine, I don't want you to do anything, that's just how it is in my house.'
>
> 'Last time I tried to tell someone, they didn't take it seriously and it just got worse.'

Children will bargain. They will want to know what the possible repercussions are before disclosing to an adult. If those repercussions pose a risk to the child, this is likely to result in them being discouraged from engaging with the process. This is where training, and to some extent experience, is important. Not getting into the minutiae too early and focusing simply on listening rather than predicting any outcome goes a long way towards reframing the conversation back to the issue.

While all schools have a safeguarding hierarchy, which may include a child protection officer, DSL, safeguarding assistant, counsellors, etc., the pupil is likely to go to a trusted adult, whether that is the class teacher, a dinner lady or the parent who comes in twice a week to read with the younger kids. So, the training and education of every single adult who interacts or has contact with children is absolutely essential.

A robust safeguarding policy also plays a key role in maintaining trust between the school, parents and the wider community. Parents need to feel confident that the school is a safe place for their children, and a clear, well-communicated safeguarding policy helps build this trust. When parents and the community are aware of the measures in place to protect children, they are more likely to engage with the school and support its efforts to create a secure environment.

Furthermore, a safeguarding policy ensures compliance with legal and regulatory requirements. Schools are obligated by law to protect pupils from harm, and a comprehensive safeguarding policy helps ensure that they meet these obligations. Failure to do so can result in legal consequences and damage the school's reputation. By adhering to a robust safeguarding policy, schools not only protect their students but also safeguard their staff and institution from potential liabilities.

A safeguarding policy is indispensable in the creation of a safe and supportive learning environment for children. It ensures that schools are proactive in preventing harm, vigilant in detecting potential risks and prepared to respond effectively to any safeguarding concerns. This comprehensive approach not only protects children but also fosters a culture of safety, trust and accountability within the school community, ultimately contributing to the overall wellbeing and success of every student.

> ## ASIDE
>
> There is nothing comfortable, enjoyable or straightforward in the handling of a safeguarding issue. Early-career teachers and experienced headteachers alike can find this one of the most uncomfortable, taxing and sometimes distressing aspects of their work. In the UK, schools are supported by a range of external agencies who can be called upon to support the case and add vital expertise and skills to the situation. In international schools, depending on the location and development of the country, the school may be responsible for the handling of the case from start to finish.
>
> In the best-case scenarios, your understanding, knowledge, intervention, training and experience contribute to the prevention or cessation of a pupil experiencing harm or abuse. The worst-case scenarios are awful to contemplate.
>
> Should you be unfamiliar with them, there is a list of historic and more up-to-date key pieces of legislation, which have contributed to the concept that we collectively call 'safeguarding' today, in Section Two, page 179.

THRIVING

... THROUGH CREATIVITY

There is an intrinsic link between a student's ability to thrive and their exposure to, and engagement in, creative pursuits. In schools, encouraging creativity within the classroom plays an essential role in enabling students to thrive emotionally, socially and academically.

All children are naturally creative but not all creativity is artistic expression. Creativity is a way of thinking, learning and approaching the world that develops a child's ability to problem-solve, innovate and promote their personal growth. By nurturing a creative environment, educators provide students with the tools to explore their individuality and environment, enhance their learning, and develop skills, passions and techniques that will serve them for a lifetime.

As teachers, we are constantly looking for ways in which we can encourage students to think and respond creatively to the learning that we are engaging them in. We know that the more creative we are in the lessons and activities we design for our students, the more engaged they are likely to be with the learning.

Students expect and deserve creative ways to engage with learning. Just search for the viral video of Jeff Bliss storming out of his class in the US when his teacher handed him yet another 'packet' of worksheets to complete as she sat passively behind her desk waiting for the end of the lesson. Jeff advocates for engaging teaching methods and speaks for most students who have suffered endless worksheet, textbook or PowerPoint modes of teaching in the past. His message to the teacher was, 'If you want us to be engaged, *you* have to be creative in how you engage us.'

When we get students being creative, it is more likely than not they will be engaged.

THE IMPORTANCE OF CREATIVITY IN EDUCATION

Creativity in the classroom is essential because it allows pupils to think beyond conventional boundaries that more traditional and one-dimensional learning activities place upon them. Tasks that are creative encourage them to question, explore and innovate in order to articulate their learning. When creativity is embraced, students develop critical-thinking skills, resilience and the confidence to face challenges with an open mind. Creative activities help students understand that there are multiple ways to solve problems, and this helps them to develop the growth mindset that we discussed in an earlier chapter ('Nurturing', pages 85–89).

We should not underestimate the importance of creative learning being 'fun'. As children get older and learning becomes more focused on exams and academic achievement, students in schools around the world will tell you that learning tends to stop being fun. In the absence of enjoyment, wonder and awe, learning becomes a chore and wellbeing can suffer as a result.

In one Year 11 English classroom, it was a surprise to see the students sitting at their desks with no books in sight. Instead, each student had a few handfuls of Lego they were carefully picking through. The task itself was a very dry grammar lesson, where the teacher was trying to show how sentences were built and how different sentence types had different constructions.

Skilfully, the teacher then introduced advanced punctuation, and the purpose of the Lego was that each colour brick related to a word class. The smaller bricks were used to show punctuation, and the students were able to visually and kinaesthetically build sentences and share them with their partners who then had to decode the bricks to write a sentence that adhered to how it had been constructed. What was clever about this lesson was the fact that students learned more from the sentences that were built incorrectly than they did from the correct structures. This activity took place in a 'nurture' group, and the students' literacy skills were very weak. The teacher creatively engaged the students while ensuring that learning was taking place at the same time. For the students, it was normal for this teacher to design creative activities in such unique ways.

Beyond academics, creativity contributes significantly to a child's thriving emotional wellbeing. Expressing ideas through expressive outlets, such as writing, drawing, music or drama, can serve as a means of emotional release and self-discovery. At a time when Arts education in the UK finds itself under increasing attack, students are suffering by being deprived of this important outlet and means of expressing themselves.

For many students, the creative arts are a vital way to process emotions and reflect on their personal experiences, yet we are seeing a decline in the numbers of students taking subjects such as art and drama at GCSE. It becomes ever more important, then, that classrooms become spaces where creativity is encouraged as often as possible to ensure students feel more engaged and connected to their creative selves, which leads to higher levels of motivation and satisfaction with learning.

SOCIAL AND EMOTIONAL BENEFITS

Creativity plays an important role in supporting emotional regulation and social skills. When students engage in creative projects, they often work collaboratively, which promotes teamwork, communication and empathy. For instance, group activities, like creating a class mural, writing a collaborative story or performing a role play or drama activity, encourage students to share ideas and listen to others. This exchange of thoughts creates a deeper sense of community and belonging within the classroom and can be applied to any subject, whether considered a creative one or not.

Creativity also allows students to explore their emotions in a safe, supportive environment. Art, for example, can be a powerful tool for children to express feelings they might struggle to articulate verbally. By channelling their emotions into creative work, students learn how to manage and make sense of their feelings. This process of emotional expression is essential for developing resilience and emotional intelligence – skills that are crucial for thriving in both school and life beyond education.

A creative classroom, where the teacher values both student wellbeing and engagement, often allows learners multiple routes to accomplish the tasks. Children thrive in an environment where they are partners in their own learning and by offering creative choices among the more traditional methods, engagement will soar and relationships will flourish. This method is particularly effective where a student has anxieties or low self-esteem in a specific subject. Allowing them to engage with the subject through non-traditional means helps to remove some of the negative emotions they may attach to it. They can then approach it using a creative skill they are more confident or proficient in.

For creativity to thrive, it needs to be actively cultivated within the classroom environment. Teachers play a key role in creating a space where creativity is celebrated and nurtured. This means designing lessons that allow for open-ended exploration rather than a fixed, predetermined outcome, providing opportunities for students to express themselves, and promoting a culture of curiosity and experimentation.

Teachers can encourage creativity by incorporating project-based learning (PBL), where students work on longer-term projects that require critical thinking, collaboration and innovation. Additionally, creating a classroom environment that is flexible and adaptable encourages students to think outside the box. Making use of creative materials, such as art supplies, craft materials and digital tools, can inspire creativity in activities or subjects that may not normally require the use of such resources and allow students to choose the medium that best suits their ideas.

ASIDE

Thriving through creativity in the class: top five tips

1. Provide students with tasks that have multiple possible solutions or outcomes. Open-ended projects allow students to explore different approaches, think critically and take creative risks. This fosters a sense of ownership and autonomy over their learning. Learning is more fun when a student and teacher can navigate a route together.
2. Use creative arts such as drawing, drama, music, podcasting, web design, blogging and creative writing in subjects like science, history and maths to help students engage with content in new and innovative ways. Integrating creative arts helps students make deeper connections to the material and express their understanding in diverse formats. This can also act as differentiation for students with additional needs.
3. Create an environment where students feel safe to share their ideas without fear of judgement. Encourage them to explore new concepts, even if they don't get it right the first time. Help students accept that mistakes are part of the learning process and that creativity flourishes through experimentation.
4. After creative projects, give students time to reflect on their process and outcomes. Ask questions like 'What did you enjoy about this project?' or 'How did your ideas evolve as you worked?'. Reflection helps students become more aware of the creative process and encourages them to continue developing creative thinking.
5. Teachers can model creative thinking by sharing their own creative interests and showing curiosity in everyday activities. Whether it's through storytelling, role play, use of multimedia or engaging in hands-on activities, demonstrating a passion for creativity will inspire students to embrace their own creative potential.

UNDERSTANDING

Understanding a pupil's wellbeing, or the wellbeing of an entire class or school, is very difficult because of the complex and abstract nature of wellbeing as a concept.

At both ends of the wellbeing spectrum, outward signs of wellbeing or illbeing can seem easy to spot. If you are familiar with the 'iceberg' models that are used to illustrate the relationship between observable and unobservable phenomena, we can apply this to a child's state of wellbeing. Underneath the observable part of the iceberg, which is the child's outward/observable appearance and state of health, their lifestyle, behaviour and sense of meaning are all the complex emotional, psychological networks and systems that contribute to that child's sense of self.

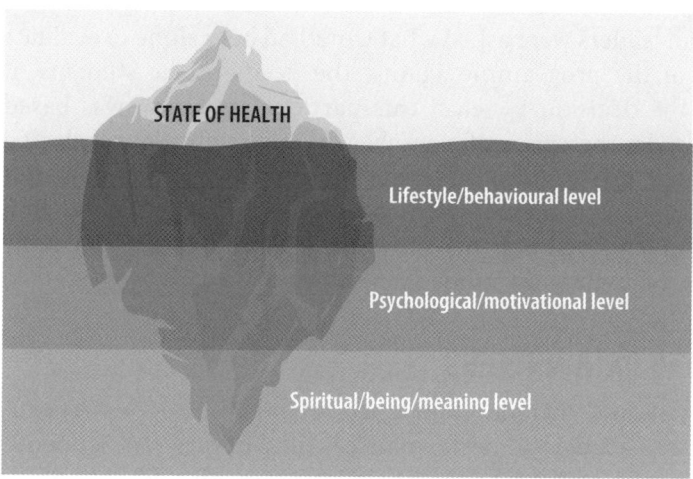

This may go some way to explaining why certain teachers are reluctant to 'do wellbeing'. Understanding the complexities of the ego, identity, trauma and healing are not what most teachers signed up for and, indeed, this is very much the realm of psychologists, mental health practitioners and therapists when a concern is identified.

So, when we seek to understand the needs of a pupil, class or school, it is important we do so from an evidence base that does not rely on observations alone. This makes the collection of wellbeing data essential for schools who prioritise wellbeing and mental health. When used effectively, data allows class teachers and pastoral leaders to identify trends, spot potential issues early and tailor interventions to meet the specific needs of students or groups. By collecting and analysing data related to these areas, schools can take a proactive approach in supporting students and ensuring their overall development.

One particular school was very proud of its RSE curriculum, which they had spent a lot of money on, as it was purchased 'off the shelf' from an established market leader in the field. It came with five-star reviews and glowing testimonies from well-known wellbeing and mental health practitioners. On first inspection, the topics and content all seemed appropriate to the age of the students (senior-school age): bullying, puberty, mental health issues, relationships, smoking/vaping, study skills and careers.

When the school leaders were asked what work had been done to evaluate the suitability of the programme against the needs of the students, it appeared that the decision to select this particular product was based on assumptions. In the space of a week, with the right data collected from the students, the pastoral leaders of the school were able to better understand what the students *really* needed from an effective RSE programme, and it turned out this 'off-the-shelf' product only partially offered the type of content the students needed.

WHY WELLBEING DATA MATTERS

Wellbeing data should include attendance records, behaviour reports, disciplinary logs, academic performance and surveys on students' feelings, relationships and mental health. By gathering this data regularly, schools can gain a holistic overview of each student's experience, rather than relying solely on anecdotal evidence or assumptions.

Schools can develop their own systems for collecting wellbeing data for no cost at all. Google and Microsoft Forms offer very simple means of collecting information, and trends and patterns can be identified in a short space of time using some very basic spreadsheet skills. There are now some incredible AI tools that can take your data and do most of the analysis for you, and many of these resources are free.

For a cost, there are more sophisticated systems available that will do all the work for you. Wellbeing platforms such as Komodo, UpStrive and YouHQ all have professionally designed surveys and built-in analytics that can be powerful tools in understanding the needs of individuals and groups better. They also allow you to benchmark your school's wellbeing health against that of others in the product's global network.

DATA-DRIVEN INTERVENTIONS

Whether your school manages its own data or uses an external platform to do the leg work, the most important step occurs after the data is collected.

Designing interventions to respond to the needs of the students is essential in maximising the impact of the data. In the many years I have been designing RSE/Enrichment curricula, I have always believed that it was important to start a new school year establishing a shared understanding of building culture and community through learning about bullying, positive relationships and team building. While this has been proven as an effective approach and a useful way to start the year, since adopting a more evidenced-based approach to constructing wellbeing programmes, it has become apparent that there is a need to revisit this topic half-way through the school year.

Group relationships go through various stages of 'forming' (coming together), 'storming' (fall outs/changes in friendships) before they are able to progress into the 'norm' (settling) and finally the 'performing' (positive and effective relationships) stage (Tuckman, 1965). In some situations, students can become stuck in or shortly after the 'storming' stage. This is particularly evident in adolescence when friendships undergo seismic shifts as children become young adults and their preferences, hobbies, habits and personalities change. They can often find themselves becoming detached from long-term childhood friends and gravitate towards others who reflect their aspirational teenage selves.

Through understanding the data, we were able to add interventions to the RSE curriculum at the appropriate times in the year to help students develop the tools to navigate changes in friendships and relationships and move forwards into the 'norm and perform' part of the model more efficiently. Without the data, we would not have been able to understand this need.

This is just one example of how understanding the data can result in better wellbeing provision but serves to reinforce the message that wellbeing provision *must* be driven by the needs of the children. If the students in your school are already feeling the pressure of exams and other academic stressors, the wisdom of using pastoral/RSE time to deliver a four-week course on study skills may need to be reconsidered. The irony that wellbeing programmes can negatively impact the wellbeing of students should not be underestimated.

WELLBEING DATA: WHOLE SCHOOL TO INDIVIDUALS

Wellbeing should be a thread that connects the students to their school and continues as they take the knowledge and skills around wellbeing into the home. When schools are effective in collecting wellbeing data, it can help them to understand how a student feels in school, at home, in their relationships and in their learning. These four areas all help teachers understand the interventions they can put in place. Wellbeing data platforms (such as Komodo), being used in many schools, are able to provide the following information:

- an overall wellbeing profile of the school
- an overall wellbeing profile of a year group
- an overall wellbeing profile of a form group
- an overall wellbeing profile of a student.

UNDERSTANDING

In the wellbeing profile of the student, pastoral leaders and the student's Head of year form tutor can see:

- their overall wellbeing score
- changes in their wellbeing score since records began
- their three highest-scoring categories (for example, 'How often have you felt motivated in the last week? – always')
- their three lowest-scoring categories (for example, 'How often do you worry about what people think about you? – always').

Having this wealth of live wellbeing data presented in this form allows all stakeholders to ensure a flexible and bespoke wellbeing provision.

Level	Understanding	Action/opportunities	Outcome
Whole school	What are the needs of the school? How do we respond?	RSE Assemblies Events Activities Student voice	The needs of the whole school are understood and met
Year group	What triggers are causing the year group to feel this way?	RSE Assemblies Review of academic pressures Explore social schisms/dynamics Student voice	The needs of the year group are understood and met
Class	What triggers are causing the class to feel this way?	Explore social schisms/dynamics Student voice 1-2-1 check-ins with students	The needs of the class are understood and met

Level	Understanding	Action/opportunities	Outcome
Student	What triggers are causing the student to feel this way?	Arrange a 1-2-1 check-in Wellbeing action plan put in place Involve parents Possible referral to external agencies Referral to school counsellor	The needs of the child are understood and met

Traditionally, whole-school wellbeing strategies have been planned and decided at the start of the year and reviewed at the end of the year. Effective use of data allows pastoral leads to review, refine and reorganise interventions constantly to meet the shifting needs of groups and individuals.

ASIDE

Many years ago, the pastoral role was a job that could be done on instinct and observation. Pastoral leads were mainly reactive to situations that occurred in their schools and intervened where problems presented themselves.

We can now operate in a much smarter way by making effective use of data in our schools, enabling us to become far more proactive than ever before. Data plays an essential role in better understanding the needs of the cohort and can alert us to issues before they become more deeply embedded.

1. **When should data be collected?** Aim to collect data on student wellbeing regularly and consistently. Surveys do run the risk of becoming a chore for students, so try to keep some key questions constant and change the focus of others to build up a more thorough profile of the students. In pastoral meetings, pull together the data you have from surveys, registers, check-ins and teacher observations.

2. **What type of data should be collected?** Aim for a mixed-methods approach. Combine quantitative data, such as attendance figures, number of incidents, wellbeing scores/ratings, with qualitative insights from conversations with the students, comments on surveys and teacher observations. A comprehensive approach such as this results in a deeper understanding of the students and interventions will be more meaningful as a result.

3. **How can students be better engaged?** Involve them in the process. Ensure they can take ownership of their wellbeing by giving them access to the data they have given you, such as their survey responses. Talk to them about what their responses say about their emotional state, what contributed to any decline/improvement and include them when deciding on which interventions may support their wellbeing best. Ask them about the surveys: what is working, what questions should we be asking and what questions don't make any sense?

4. **Should we include safeguarding data**? Yes, absolutely, but adhere to your school's GDPR policy and ensure that only those with the appropriate access can see the safeguarding information you have on a student. Include incidents related to bullying, inappropriate language, physical incidents/fighting and use this data to create a safer school environment. Use student council and student voice to better understand where your students feel most vulnerable and intervene as necessary.

5. **What next? Evaluate, evaluate, evaluate!** Keep referring back to the data and student feedback to assess the effectiveness of your wellbeing programmes and interventions. Look for changes that occur after implementing any measures and celebrate your successes with your community by using this as evidence of its impact.

VOICE

'The child shall have the right to freedom of expression; this right shall include freedom to seek, receive and impart information and ideas of all kinds, regardless of frontiers, either orally, in writing or in print, in the form of art, or through any other media of the child's choice.'

Article 13, UN Convention on the Rights of the Child, 1990

As well as being 'great wellbeing practice', the right for every child to have a voice is included in the guidelines drawn up by the United Nations in 1989 ('Convention on the Rights of the Child'), a treaty that was ratified or accepted by 196 countries and came into force in September 1990.

'Student voice' refers to the active participation of students in decision-making processes within a school: from recruitment decisions right down to which flavour juices should be sold in the tuck shop.

Student voice empowers children to express their opinions, ideas and perspectives on issues that affect their learning environment and overall school experience. When students feel heard and valued, it has a direct and positive impact on their wellbeing, leading to a more inclusive, respectful and nurturing school community. You would be hard pushed to find a school that does not operate a formalised system of student voice in one shape or another, from student councils, student-led projects, student surveys and other feedback channels.

Student voice (sometimes referred to as 'learner voice' when the feedback sought is specifically about teaching and learning in some contexts) can also operate informally. There should be frequent opportunities throughout the day for a student to have their voice heard. Mindful that not all students may have the courage to speak directly to an adult, a school should carefully consider the different avenues and platforms available for a student to express how they feel.

As digital natives, many students may feel more comfortable giving their opinion via an online system or app. In its simplest form, take the example of an outstanding teacher who would end his lessons by giving students a quiet minute to email him directly with any thoughts, feelings, questions or issues about the lesson. Being the inspiring teacher that he was, 90% of the emails he received were from students practising gratitude, as they thanked the teacher for the lesson or shared their excitement about what was being learned. As nice as that 90% may be for his ego, it was the information the teacher received from the other 10% that was most useful.

Students felt safe giving feedback in this confidential manner, and the teacher was able to tailor his lessons and relationships with each student over the course of the year as a result of the feedback received.

> 'Thanks for the lesson, I am finding this quite hard.'
>
> 'Please don't be mad at me – I didn't finish because I was tired today.'
>
> 'Don't say anything to David, he's my best friend, but he keeps messing around when you aren't looking.'

These simple emails made a positive impact in so many of the areas we have already covered: atmosphere, behaviour, engagement and relationships. When students are encouraged to voice their thoughts and ideas in this way, they feel more in control of their learning experience. Learning feels more like a partnership with the teacher, as the student has a more active role. This sense of ownership promotes a feeling of empowerment, as students see that their contributions are not only heard but also acted upon.

It must be stressed, however, that if the feedback is *not* acted upon, the activity is pointless and, while it might impress an observer, your headteacher or an inspector, the students will be deflated and become disillusioned by the lack of any action taken as a result of their feedback. It will become a gimmick. Empowerment is a key factor in promoting wellbeing, as it builds self-confidence and encourages autonomy.

Students who feel that they have some control of their environment are far more likely to engage meaningfully with their education, positively influencing both their academic performance and emotional wellbeing.

RELATIONSHIPS AND RESILIENCE

Teachers who truly listen to their students and give them a voice will be rewarded with the students' trust and faith. Positive relationships with teachers, tutors and among adults as colleagues are essential to whole-school wellbeing.

When a student has a positive relationship with the adults in a school, they are more likely to respond positively, take onboard advice and rise to challenges. These are essential in helping the student build resilience. When a child responds to an adult out of fear, and student voice is denied, resilience is negatively impacted and their performance/progress will be restricted. Teachers are motivators and the most successful teachers get the best out of their students because, in addition to their excellent subject knowledge and pedagogy, they can motivate to such an extent that the student wants to achieve because of their relationship with the teacher.

Teacher voice is as essential to relationships as student voice! Bookshelves are awash with books on leadership, from army commanders to famous sports team managers, and a common theme that runs through these leaders is their ability to get the best out of people. Leaders know what makes people tick and teachers are no different because we are, after all, leaders in our classrooms.

Good teachers have the ability to motivate, encourage and give students the boost they need to complete a task or activity. By doing so, they provide lessons in resilience and thereby positively impact the students' wellbeing. The lazy teacher accepts when a student is defeated and reinforces negative messages within them as a result: you can't do it, you are not good enough, there is no point in trying. Communication and voice are key.

VOICE, DIVERSITY AND INCLUSION

Student voice is a great tool for ensuring that inclusivity and diversity are effectively embedded in your school. Encouraging student voice allows teachers and leaders to identify and address issues related to inclusivity, such as unequal representation, cultural misunderstandings, discrimination and feelings of isolation among certain student groups. By seeking input from all students, especially those from minority or marginalised groups, schools and pastoral leaders can better understand the unique challenges these students face.

This leads to more informed decision-making and the development, implementation or review of policies that reflect the diverse needs of the student body. Student voice ensures that initiatives aimed at promoting diversity are not top-down mandates, but rather collaborative efforts that involve the very students they are intended to benefit. The same students are best placed to tell you whether your planned event or initiative is going to go down a storm in the playground, or be a complete flop!

When students from all walks of life see that their voices are heard and respected, they feel a greater sense of belonging and connection. The school starts becoming a place where everyone shares responsibility for its direction. This is especially important for students from underrepresented backgrounds, who may otherwise feel excluded or overlooked in school environments. Promoting student voice helps break down barriers, allowing for more equitable participation, collaboration and representation.

In addition, encouraging diverse voices helps educate the entire school community about different cultures, identities and perspectives. It nurtures empathy, tolerance and respect among students, creating a more inclusive atmosphere where differences are celebrated rather than marginalised.

Ultimately, student voice empowers young people to be agents of change in their own learning environments. By giving all students a platform to express themselves, schools can create a more-inclusive, diverse and supportive community where every student feels valued and understood.

ASIDE

Student voice: five tips

1. **Ensure students feel comfortable and respected when sharing their thoughts.** Use anonymous feedback methods like suggestion boxes, online apps or digital surveys for those who may be hesitant to speak up in front of peers. Establish a classroom culture where every opinion is valued, and students feel secure in expressing their views. Make sure that any changes that are made to school practices or policies are communicated with the students so they know their voice has been heard and action has been taken.

2. **Actively involve students in school and classroom decisions, from event planning to setting classroom rules.** When students see that their input leads to real changes, they feel more invested and engaged in their learning environment. In one school I visited, there was a display board in the main Reception area, visible to all, that had two columns, 'You said/We did', which highlighted all the suggestions made by students and parents and all the changes that were made as a result. A superb piece of PR!

3. **Not all students are comfortable with traditional methods of communication.** Offer diverse ways to share feedback, such as digital apps, small-group discussions or visual tools like mood boards or charts. Catering to different communication styles will ensure a more inclusive engagement. Don't underestimate the power of the humble sticky note. Having students write their feedback on a sticky note and sticking it on the board on their way out as their exit ticket is simple but effective — and can be anonymous (depending on how well you know your students' handwriting!).

4. **Make student voice a routine part of your classroom by conducting regular check-ins.** These could be weekly reflections, quick exit tickets at the end of class or mid-term surveys about how students feel about their learning experience. Consistency in gathering feedback keeps the dialogue ongoing and relevant. Practice makes perfect and students will rise to the challenge and give more-specific and pertinent feedback when this is a regular activity.
5. **Show students that their voices lead to action.** After receiving their input, communicate the changes or improvements you plan to make, and explain why some suggestions may not be feasible. Transparency builds trust and encourages students to continue participating. Share the most useful or well-articulated pieces of feedback with the class so they know what good feedback looks like. Use SMART (specific, measurable, achievable, relevant, timely) targets as a guide on how to give specific feedback with younger students.

WELCOMES

Welcomes are so important in a whole variety of social and organisational contexts that we almost take them for granted and forget the role they play in establishing connections and making those important first impressions.

We are hardwired and bound by codes of social conduct to commence all interactions with a welcome or an introduction in most aspects of our lives, so it is easy to overlook the importance of this in the context of a school. Parents/visitors to a school can often tell whether a school is welcoming within minutes of being on site.

This is why school leaders pay close attention to logistics such as:

- the arrival procedures at the school gates;
- the presentation and location of reception;
- the behaviour, appearance and knowledge of reception staff (an incredibly important job as the first customer-facing representatives of the school that most visitors meet);
- the displays in the school's reception and facilities;
- the comfort of places where parents/visitors wait;
- and the behaviour and traffic of students through the reception/ waiting area.

What is it like entering your school as a stranger for the first time? Take the walk from outside the school grounds to your school reception and look at it through the eyes of a stranger.

Let us also consider the welcomes we afford our students at these key milestones of the school year and, indeed, of their lives.

NEW SCHOOL YEAR

Excellent wellbeing practice is to welcome students back to the new school year with positivity and excitement. Most schools will greet their students and parents at the gate and it is common practice for senior school leaders to take on this duty.

The first day of a new school year is usually the time when the school sets out its stall on the strategic priorities for the year ahead, in student-friendly language appropriate to the age of your students, of course. There is an important opportunity, even in these first few hours of the school year, to re-establish the norms of behaviour expected of students. At this stage, students should be reminded of where to go for support if they need it. Names, faces and locations of key pastoral staff should be shared and this should operate as a reminder to returning students and ensure students new to the school have someone to go to right from their first hour or two in their new school.

Most schools do not rush into 'normal lessons' until students have been sufficiently welcomed and important information has been shared with them. The start to a new year sets the tone for the rest of the year and getting students prepared and in the right mindset is an important part of the process.

It is important to consider parents at this stage too. What information do they need ahead of the first day of school? The welcome-back-to-school message should begin before school opens on day one to ensure that even the most disorganised of parents are able to support their children in having a successful first day back to school. Reminders about uniform, equipment, mobile phones, lunchtime arrangements, PE/swimming, and any other administrative or logistical details that may make some parents or students anxious, should be shared upfront.

Teachers will also be vigilant at this stage of any changes or signs that all is not well with a pupil. This can be challenging, especially as in some instances, the class will be new to you if the pupils have moved up a year and they are previously unknown to you. Effective handover documents and conversations with the pupil's previous class or form teacher may prepare you to some extent, but any signs of concern should be raised, checked and triaged rather than left to chance as you get to know the pupil better.

NEW SCHOOL TERM

While nowhere near as exciting or anxiety-inducing as the first day of the school year, the new school term also marks an important stage in the life cycle of the school year and, therefore, a pupil's development. Spending time talking to the class about their experiences of the winter/spring holidays is a positive and gentle welcome back to the new school term, regardless of the age of the students.

It is effective wellbeing and safeguarding practice to follow up privately with the pupil who has little to say, who didn't enjoy the break or is teary and upset. Two/three weeks off school can be a long time for children, so those reminders about kindness and where to go if help or support is needed help reinforce the importance of student wellbeing as each new term begins.

In the school's first communication to parents of the term, it is helpful to remind parents to inform you of any changes in family circumstances, a pupil's health, friendships, mood, etc., so the pupil can be supported from the earliest possible time. While to a parent, it may not seem like the loss of a pet dog has much bearing on the child's enjoyment and progress at school, we know this can be absolutely devastating to a child, so a reminder may just result in that little nugget of information you need to get the support and care to those who need it most.

THE SCHOOL DAY

Now the school term is up and running, routines are established and, for staff and students, one day can feel very much like the next if variety and engagement are lacking. How depressing! In a school and classroom where wellbeing is prioritised, students are met at the school gate or the classroom door on arrival. Some students may need reassurances that today is a fresh start, particularly if the previous day was a challenging one. For others, you may be the only person that day who asks how they are. If you see the same group of children each day, remembering and asking about something that is important to them helps reinforce positive relationships: 'How did tennis practice go last night?', 'I saw that your football team won again!', 'I hope you are feeling better after that tummy ache yesterday?'.

Students are more inclined to engage with a teacher who knows them and cares about them. Ten minutes spent meeting, greeting and chatting (seemingly idly) is ten minutes well spent and should be seen as a benefit to learning, not a distraction from it.

START OF THE LESSON

With students sufficiently welcomed, we are now beginning the process of introducing the learning. Whether this is a new activity or concept or a continuation of something previously started, students want to be re-engaged and re-energised. Weaker students may desperately need that all-important recap in order to access the learning.

Learning games that require knowledge recall are perfect for introducing or recapping learning. Digital tools (Kahoot!, Blooket, Quizizz) are particularly powerful for this as they can 'gamify' the process, while at the same time protecting and highlighting those weaker students without fear of them being exposed. A great way to 'flip' this activity is to have the class compete as a team against you as the teacher, so they have to pool and share their knowledge against you. When students are introduced to learning in a way that engages and excites them, we are calling upon their hedonic happiness to temporarily engage them in a way that smooths the transition from starter to main activity positively and effectively.

TRANSITION POINTS

As children move through school, they will, of course, encounter a number of transition points. In a UK school, these include: Early Years Foundation Stage (EYFS) to key stage (KS) 1, KS1 to KS2, junior school to senior school, KS3 to KS4, and senior school to sixth form or college. While these are formalised by age and the chronological progression through school, other transition points are less formalised or acknowledged. The transition through puberty, navigating sexuality, becoming sexually aware/active, moving schools or moving homes, vaping/smoking/drugs, loss and grief, changes to the family set up, (such as divorce, marriage, new siblings) are all huge milestones in the life of a young person.

A school that practises outstanding wellbeing has plans and programmes in place for all of these transition points. Furthermore, parents are aware of them well in advance of their child encountering them and, in the case of the more sensitive personal transition points, these are planned and delivered by those with the specific responsibility and experience. In more sensitive cases, the expertise of external services can be called upon.

ASIDE

Welcomes are important for the whole school community. They serve multiple purposes:

1. **They create a positive first impression.** Is this a place you would want to send your children? Is this a place an adult new to the school would want to work?
2. **They build relationships.** We gravitate naturally towards people who we feel care for us. A welcome is a sign of care. When we feel cared for, we are more likely to comply and engage with that person.
3. **They promote inclusivity.** As teachers, we have no 'favourites', of course. A welcome that includes all students reinforces how important each and every one of those students is to us and creates an atmosphere where everyone feels able to contribute.
4. **They reduce anxiety**. To repeat a key point from our chapter on atmosphere, a friendly and positive atmosphere reduces anxiety by setting a mood and tone that enables the student to feel safe and comfortable as they acknowledge your positive and friendly mood.
5. **Modelling/expectations.** When students see you welcoming and accepting everyone, this sets the tone for how members of the class are expected to treat one another. You are modelling care and kindness from the moment they enter your space.

How does your school measure up?

1. Consider following up with adults who have visited your school for the first time. Ask them whether they felt welcomed and what contributed to their experience.
2. What follow-up do you have in place for students new to your school? How effective is your buddy programme? How is the experience of a new starter shared with pastoral staff so improvements can be made?
3. Are the students in your school aware of their role in ensuring that the school is a welcoming place for children, other adults and visitors? How do you prepare them for acting in a kind and supportive way?
4. Welcomes are no longer just 'in-person' interactions. How welcoming are your school website and social media channels?
5. How much time is given to mapping key transition points on the calendar for each academic year? What strategies are in place to prepare and integrate students in formal, informal and personal milestones?

XERCISING

... MINDFULNESS

Wellbeing practices need to be exercised regularly in order to strengthen and embed them. This is particularly true of practices that are new or suffer from a certain degree of misunderstanding.

Today's children and young people are living in a fast-paced, digital world where stress and distraction are common problems. Mindfulness is increasingly coming into the foreground as an effective approach in addressing these challenges by teaching young people skills around focus, stress management and emotional resilience. Exercising school-wide mindfulness can be a powerful tool that supports mental health as well as academic behaviour and social harmony.

Yet mindfulness, like many aspects of wellbeing, does suffer from a lack of understanding of its core principles by those unfamiliar with the concept.

One common misconception about mindfulness is that it's simply about 'clearing your mind' or achieving a state of complete calm, which can make it seem intimidating or unattainable. The aim isn't to lull your class into a zen-like state. Mindfulness isn't about getting rid of thoughts, but about noticing them without getting caught up in them. Some people also believe mindfulness is only for relaxation, but it's really about being present and aware at any moment, whether it's a stressful one or a calm one.

Another reason mindfulness can get too easily dismissed by the uninitiated is the misconception that it takes a lot of time or needs to be done through formal meditation, when it can be as simple as taking a few deep breaths or focusing on a daily activity like eating or walking. Even those who view mindfulness as a positive tool can oversimplify it as a quick fix for stress or anxiety, but the reality is that it's more about building long-term emotional resilience and awareness, which requires regular practice and patience.

This is by no means a silver bullet or something that will come naturally and easily to all. Instead, it is another tool to have in your wellbeing toolbox and something to consider if you have not yet had a chance to put it into practice.

Mindfulness then, simply put, is the practice of paying attention to the present moment, non-judgmentally and with intention. It allows individuals to become aware of their thoughts, feelings and sensations as they happen, without getting caught up in them. For students, cultivating this skill can be incredibly beneficial, helping them to manage anxiety, increase focus and improve their overall wellbeing.

BASIC MINDFULNESS

Despite the increased attention and focus on wellbeing in the last few years, mindfulness does not seem to have taken off at the same rate. In some schools, it may operate as an ECA and, at best, a small pocket of teachers in a school may practise it as part of their classroom routines. It is still rare to see schools adopt whole-school practices to mindfulness, though as anxiety rates continue to rise in young people, sooner or later attention will turn to the powerful benefits this offers.

For those who are unfamiliar with mindfulness, the best starting point is to look at the basics in the first instance. These techniques are low risk, require little to no experience or training and can be supported by resources readily available on YouTube or the internet.

One of the easiest ways is through mindful breathing. Begin by asking the students to sit comfortably, close their eyes and take deep breaths. Guide them to focus on their breath as it moves in and out, encouraging them to notice how it feels without trying to change it. Even just a minute or two can help them centre their attention.

Take a look at the video resources available on YouTube by @The Mindfulness Teacher. These videos are aesthetically pleasing for younger students, have activities in a variety of lengths covering different types of breathing techniques, and take all the work away from you by having a guided narration or written instructions to accompany the activity. For teens and young adults, look at the free resources online and on YouTube offered by Headspace or The Anna Freud Foundation.

Another simple activity is a body scan, in which you guide students to focus on different parts of their body, starting with their toes and working up to their head, noticing any sensations. This helps the students become more aware of their bodies and encourages relaxation. While this is an activity best carried out in a lesson or space where the person can lie flat, it can also be successfully practised by resting your head on folded arms in front of you on the table. The teacher acts as narrator, guiding the students through a tour or 'scan' of their body. There is a transcript to assist you in this activity in Section Two (pages 181–182).

Mindful listening is also effective in grounding and centring a student's focus and attention. Ask the students to close their eyes and listen to the sounds around them for a minute or two. Afterwards, they can share what they noticed, which helps them focus on the present moment. They should be encouraged to share how what they noticed made them feel. How often does a child (or an adult for that matter) stop everything and engage with the basics of their environment in this way? This is a beautiful activity to do out on the school field on a warm day and a simple way to develop the character strength of 'appreciation of beauty'.

Mindful colouring or drawing is another fun way to introduce mindfulness. Encourage students to focus entirely on the colours, lines and patterns they are creating, paying attention to the experience without worrying about the outcome.

This is most successful where the purpose of the activity and the focus on 'being present' is understood by the participants. Discuss, and make it explicit, how the students felt before (get them to write it on a sticky note and stick it on the board) and after (students should go back to their note and write down how they feel now). Encouraging students to keep a mindfulness journal is a great way to integrate mindfulness into daily routines. Students can write about their emotions, challenges or what they observed during mindfulness exercises. This practice promotes reflection and self-awareness, both of which are key components of emotional wellbeing. Teachers can guide students by providing prompts such as, 'How did you feel after today's mindfulness exercise?' or 'What thoughts or feelings did you notice during our mindful breathing session?'.

Lastly, mindful movement, like simple stretches or yoga poses, can help students connect with their bodies and bring their attention to how they feel physically. Even basic stretches or slow movements paired with deep breathing can be very grounding for kids. This can be done in a classroom, in a larger space like a hall or gym, or outdoors.

Again, there are thousands of YouTube videos that can support you through this. Don't be afraid to approach this as a newbie with the class. Navigating it together as beginners and showing your willingness to learn and engage with a new practice is a fantastic way to model a positive attitude to learning. Check out 'Cosmic Kids Yoga' on YouTube. The activities take a fun approach to mindful movement and the videos are produced to a very high quality and are themed around characters, films and games that appeal to children such as Moana, Mario Kart, Animal Crossing and The Little Mermaid, to name but a few.

ASIDE

Xercising mindfulness

Mindfulness can be introduced in a classroom without it even being referred to in the first instance as 'mindfulness'. All of the activities above can be used as games or 'brain breaks' where you feel the pupils would benefit from a short distraction from learning.

- Guide your class and explain what you are doing and why you are doing it.
- Discuss the impact of the activity afterwards and how it made the pupils feel.
- Inquire how they might use this outside of the class/school and encourage them to share success stories of practising mindfulness out of school.

- As pupils become more comfortable and confident with mindfulness, encourage them to be independent in the need to identify mindful moments.
- Not all mindful moments need to be whole-class moments. The agitated child, the anxious child and the distracted child might all benefit from space and time to put these techniques into practice without the whole class having to be involved.
- Using teaching assistants or having a quiet place in the classroom for this can be really beneficial.

With the passing of time, and as the different strategies and techniques are added to the students' skill set, they will start to become more aware of which techniques work best for them in different situations, as will you. The vigilant teacher is always on the lookout for that clever customer in the class who will 'try it on' by requesting a mindful moment to go and colour in when in actual fact they want to avoid today's geography test.

Mindfulness should help focus on learning, not take time away from it.

YOU

Are you old enough to remember the classic recruitment advert for teachers in the 2000s: 'Those who can, teach.'? It was an inspirational and empowering little soundbite for those thinking of joining the industry. However, it is interesting to note that they decided to put a comma after the word 'can'. Left open as a sentence to complete, and if the advert had been completely honest, whole generations of future teachers might have been put off entirely with a dose of reality:

Those who can, *plan lessons in the evening.*

Those who can, *mark work in bed at night.*

Those who can, *worry about the welfare of their pupils at the weekend.*

Those who can, *sometimes buy their own classroom supplies.*

Those who can, *miss out on some of their own children's school events and milestones.*

Those who can, *are under constant pressure to hit key metrics.*

Those who can, *are pawns in government point-scoring.*

Those who can, *have to – even when they feel they can't.*

Those who can, *often can't at the weekend because they are so tired.*

Feel free to add your own. It makes for a fun staffroom game at the end of term! Teacher wellbeing is, of course, essential to a thriving educational environment. When teachers are in good physical, emotional and mental health, they are better equipped to inspire and educate their students. Physically and mentally healthy teachers are more engaged, energetic and capable of providing high-quality instruction. Their positive state of mind and resilience can significantly influence the school culture, creating a supportive and nurturing environment for everyone.

You, in your classroom, at your best, are a thing of beauty. You run that classroom like a demi-god. You have pupils eating out of the palm of your hand and those 'Eureka!' moments are being experienced (by those lucky enough to be in your room) left, right and centre. At least that's what the teaching adverts would have you believe. The reality is that many of us sacrifice our own wellbeing at the drop of a hat in favour of all the other priorities, tasks, duties and your own family responsibilities that compete for our time.

Without a doubt, those teachers who manage to maintain good wellbeing are more likely to have long, fulfilling careers that help reduce the high turnover rates that many schools face. Teacher retention is crucial, not only for maintaining continuity and stability within the school community, but also for reducing the financial and administrative burdens associated with recruiting and training new staff.

Healthy teachers can manage stress better and avoid burnout, which leads to fewer absences and a more consistent learning experience for students. A teacher's wellbeing directly impacts their effectiveness and creativity, and their ability to build strong, positive relationships with students, colleagues and parents. Thus, fostering teacher wellbeing is not just beneficial, but essential for the overall success of the educational system.

DO WE PRACTISE WHAT WE PREACH?

I hope there was some 'nodding along' as you read the opening section to this chapter. Most teachers would recognise the importance of their own wellbeing while acknowledging that it often appears very low down on their list of priorities. Why is this? Perhaps it feels too selfish to abandon the marking and the lesson planning to engage in some self-care, which will only cause us more anxiety as we rue an hour of precious planning time lost in favour of something more self-indulgent. Some of the most common reasons we sacrifice our own wellbeing include:

- **Workload and time constraints**. Many of us face overwhelming workloads, with long hours spent planning lessons, marking and meeting administrative demands. This leaves little time for self-care activities. The stakes are too high – 'stuff' has to 'get done'.

- **Cultural norms and expectations**. The teaching profession is often characterised by a culture of selflessness and sacrifice. Teachers may feel guilty or selfish for taking time for themselves, believing they should always prioritise their students' needs above all else.
- **Lack of resources and support**. Many schools do not provide adequate resources or support systems for teacher wellbeing. Without institutional support, it becomes challenging for teachers to find and utilise wellbeing resources effectively.
- **Stress and burnout**. Chronic stress and burnout can create a vicious cycle: teachers feel too exhausted to engage in wellbeing practices and this, in turn, exacerbates their stress and burnout. It is a huge threat to the profession.
- **Perfectionism and high standards**. Teachers often hold themselves to very high standards and may feel that they need to be perfect in their roles. This perfectionism can prevent them from taking breaks or seeking help when needed.

Take the word 'teacher' out of this and now imagine these were issues being faced by a child or young person in your care. What would your advice be? We would insist on a clear plan that included specific strategies to correct or reduce these pressures. We would provide advice, resources and support and, where possible, lighten the load.

Yet, for some reason, we are unable to practise what we preach as professionals when it comes to ourselves and our colleagues. Addressing these barriers is crucial for helping teachers take greater care with their own wellbeing. Schools must create environments that encourage and support teacher self-care and provide practical solutions to help teachers manage their wellbeing.

Ultimately, the role of schools and the role of a teacher have changed dramatically over the last 50 years. Relationships put more strain on our wellbeing now than at any other time in the history of education. Relationships with leaders can often be emotionally fraught as the leaders themselves try to manage their own burden of expectations. The dynamics between school and home have also changed significantly in recent years. Parents have higher expectations than they did 20 years ago; they hold the school and individual teachers to account more frequently.

Many parents have found themselves more anxious than ever about their child's wellbeing in the post-Covid landscape, and those anxieties can manifest themselves in the form of frustration directed towards the school and individual teachers. The shift in family dynamics, including the rise in the number of blended families, has impacted the role of a teacher, as they increasingly find themselves cast in the role of a caregiver. Finally, the young people themselves are changing. Teaching is now more concerned with ensuring that students know how to 'be', not just know how to 'know'. The net result of these changes is increased stress and expectations on the humble class teacher who has had more added to their load and very little taken away.

TEACHER WELLBEING IN THE UK

Understanding the scope of teacher-wellbeing issues requires looking at the data. Here are some key statistics from the UK that highlight the state of teacher wellbeing and the challenges the profession faces:

- According to a 2024 survey by the Teachers' Union (the NASUWT), 84% of teachers have experienced work-related stress, with over three-quarters describing their stress levels as high or very high. (Available at: www.nasuwt.org.uk/news/campaigns/teacher-wellbeing-survey.html)
- Research by Education Support in 2022 found that 72% of teachers described themselves as stressed and 58% reported that they had considered leaving the profession due to the pressures of the job. (Available at: www.educationsupport.org.uk/media/zoga2r13/teacher-wellbeing-index-2022.pdf)
- The Education Support Partnership reported that 77% of teachers experienced mental health issues due to their work, with anxiety and depression being the most prevalent conditions. (Available at: www.educationsupport.org.uk/resources/for-organisations/research/teacher-wellbeing-index/)
- A study conducted by York St John University (2024) found that teacher burnout was consistently associated with physical

symptoms such as headaches, illnesses such as gastroenteritis, and inflammation. (Available at: www.researchgate.net/publication/369600942_Teacher_burnout_and_physical_health_A_systematic_review)

- Data from the Department for Education indicated that in 2022, one in three new teachers left the profession within the first five years, highlighting significant retention challenges linked to wellbeing concerns. (Available at: www.sec-ed.co.uk/content/news/another-year-and-another-40-000-teachers-quit-the-chalkface/)

These statistics underscore the urgent need for comprehensive strategies to improve teacher wellbeing in the UK, highlighting the widespread nature of the problem and its implications for the education sector.

ASIDE

Your own personal wellbeing

Whether or not your school and its leaders actively promote teacher wellbeing, you would be well advised to take proactive steps to manage your own wellbeing by incorporating practical and sustainable practices into your daily routines. If your school does not currently have a staff wellbeing committee, start one and collaborate in putting some of these ideas into practice.

1. Regular mindfulness and meditation practices can help reduce stress and improve mental clarity. Apps like Headspace and Calm offer guided sessions tailored for busy schedules.
2. Incorporating physical activity into the day, even in short bursts, can significantly enhance physical and mental health. This can include walking during breaks, doing some stretching exercises or participating in a fitness class after school with a willing and motivational PE teacher/department leading the way!

3. Maintaining a balanced diet with nutritious meals can boost energy levels and overall health. Preparing healthy snacks and staying hydrated throughout the day are simple yet effective steps. Have healthy-eating days, 'pot-luck' lunches and other fun, food-related activities in the staffroom to boost morale and get the school together.
4. Setting clear boundaries between work life and personal life is crucial. Teachers should designate specific times for work and personal activities, ensuring they have time to relax and recharge.
5. Engaging in professional development that focuses on stress management and resilience can provide teachers with tools and techniques to handle stress more effectively.
6. Build a strong support network with colleagues who can offer emotional support and practical advice. Regularly scheduled meetings or informal gatherings can help teachers share experiences and strategies for wellbeing.
7. Accessing mental health resources, such as counselling services, employee-assistance programmes or mental health days, can provide essential support. Schools should ensure these resources are easily accessible.
8. Practising self-compassion and understanding that it is okay to take breaks and seek help is vital. Teachers should remind themselves that looking after their own wellbeing is not only beneficial for them but also for their students and the entire school community.
9. Beware of staffroom toxicity. While it may bring temporary relief to have a good moan over a cup of tea with your colleagues — and, in small doses, sharing your frustrations with like-minded colleagues does indeed share the burden — be mindful not to become too deeply entrenched in the systemic toxicity that can be a feature of some staffrooms. This only breeds longer-term resentments and clouds your ability to see the positives.

10. Gratitude! Don't forget to be conscious of those moments of success, beauty, connection and joy. They are there. Don't let them pass you by. Create a folder for the nice emails you get from students and parents, and have a physical folder for the cards and gifts you receive. Go back to these when you are feeling like you can't remember why you do the job. No doubt you will find plenty of reminders in the gratitude others have shown you over the years.

By adopting these practices, teachers can create a healthier and more-balanced lifestyle, which will, in turn, enhance their effectiveness and satisfaction in their professional and personal lives. Schools and leaders must support these efforts by fostering a culture that values and promotes teacher wellbeing.

ZZZ

... THE POWER OF SLEEP

As science and data combine to make us more informed about student wellbeing, we are now in a position to better understand more about the key factors that contribute to positive wellbeing. If you were asked to rank which of the following affects a child's wellbeing the most, what would you put at the top of the list?

- Social media
- Academic stress/pressure
- Relationships
- Physical health
- Sleep
- Nutrition
- Parenting
- School

We are now seeing more and more data and research that identifies sleep as the major contributing factor to the wellbeing of young people.

Komodo, a wellbeing-data-management system, collects and analyses global data from its users, obtained from over one million surveys conducted in 22 countries. Its annual report shows sleep as the number one area of concern. Sleep is the cornerstone that impacts on all the other items in the list above. There exists a particularly problematic relationship between social media and sleep; a relationship that is interdependent. Children who do not have boundaries in place around their social media habits at night can find their sleeping patterns affected.

Not only can screen time affect the quality of sleep – as a result of exposure to the blue-light frequencies that alter the body's natural production of the hormone melatonin – socialising online, gaming and accessing inappropriate or negative social media content do not contribute to a nighttime routine that aims for a calm and positive end to the day.

The quality of a person's sleep underpins their behaviour, attitude and mood for the rest of the day. Poor decisions are made by a sleep-deprived child, focus and engagement suffer, patience and tolerance are in short supply which can, in turn, affect the development of healthy relationships with peers, teachers and parents. According to the Great Ormond Street Hospital website, children need between 8 and 12 hours of sleep a night, yet it is not uncommon, especially in a secondary-school environment, to speak to young people who sleep for fewer than 6 hours a night on a regular basis. More often than not, the reason for the lack of sleep is, of course, technology: gaming or social media.

SLEEP HYGIENE

It can be very difficult for schools to have an impact on the sleeping habits of their pupils. Like much of what we try to achieve with our wellbeing programmes, we can lead the horse to water, but we cannot make it drink. But reinforcing the importance of sleep hygiene, providing awareness, education, skills and tools is our first line of defence. Parent workshops should prioritise the importance of sleep on wellbeing, as there may be a lack of understanding of how insufficient sleep can be a fertile ground for a whole range of other problems.

When exploring the behaviour concerns of a student, their sleep habits should be understood. It can be difficult approaching parents with concerns about a child's sleeping habits, as some may see this as an affront to their parenting or an invasion of the privacy around their homelife. But children are skilled in the dark arts of tricking the adults around them about their night-time routines, and parents may actually be unaware of the full extent of the problem unless it is raised as an issue.

There are teenagers out there who have a spare smartphone, for example, ready for those times when their parents confiscate their primary device.

It is now possible to access social media apps and websites on smart TVs, gaming consoles and even smart watches. Parents are up against it when they try to instil healthy night-time routines in their children, and it should not be assumed that the tired child is a result of bad parenting.

THE HORMONAL TIME SHIFT

Children and teenagers love sleep – but not at the times we want them to sleep. Try putting a teen to bed at a ridiculously early hour such as 8pm ('ridiculous' to them, completely reasonable for us adults, of course) and there can be all sorts of drama and histrionics. Sleep is not important to them at this time. Now fast forward until wake-up time, and sleep all of a sudden becomes their life blood; they can't get enough of it. How unfair it is to wake them up at 11am at the weekend!

Routine is essential. Parents are so good at this with babies and toddlers. It is almost a religion to us as we feed, bathe, dress, soothe, read to and settle our little ones literally by clockwork. Most of us manage to sustain this through childhood, albeit with some minor changes to the routine as our babies become bigger kids, and then somehow it disintegrates as soon as those kids of ours become teens. To the teen, the later the night, the bigger the badge of honour – particularly among their peers. Sleeping early is not cool and many adults see this as a form of rebellion.

In actual fact, science shows us that in adolescence, teens undergo a hormonal time shift which can propel the internal body clock forward by one or two hours. Going to battle with a hormonal teenager and trying to force them to sleep at a time when their brains are telling them 'you are not tired' is a battle likely to be lost. A smarter battle to pick for parents might be in relation to the habits and hygiene around what happens in that newfound hour or two. This is where schools can support and reinforce what is hopefully being practised at home.

ASIDE

A checklist to share with parents

1. Establish a set schedule and consistent times around the night-time rituals.
2. Have a to-do list around the night-time routine: eating, homework, bath/shower, deadline for phone use, reading or listening to a podcast, TV time – including off time, lights down/lights off, etc.
3. The temperature in the room is important, although personal preferences vary; the average ideal bedroom temperature is believed to be 19–20 degrees Celsius.
4. Dim lights after dark. This is essential to enable our body's circadian rhythm (or internal clock) to understand the stage of the cycle it should be in. Bright lights or blue lights from electronic devices mess with this body clock and this is the primary reason we experience poor sleep quality.
5. Unplug an hour before bed. Turn phones and screens off one hour before the time when sleep should be kicking in. Even adults should resist the temptation to check phones by having them on charge out of the room. Where it is not possible to have the phone out of the room, a compromise would be to have it on 'do not disturb' mode, so the Snapchat and WhatsApp notifications are silenced.
6. Avoid stimulants in the late afternoon/early evening. Coke, coffee and energy drinks are going to fizz up the activity in a child's brain and are to be avoided at all costs.
7. Avoid afternoon naps. There is a natural slump that can occur as children come home from school, especially for teens, and the temptation can be to sleep right through to the next morning. Oversleep can be as damaging as too little sleep and this should be avoided.
8. Ending the day with a grounding or positive activity, such as a breathing technique, a gratitude journal or a meditative podcast, paves the way for a pleasant onward journey into dreamland.

CODA: GOODNIGHT AND GOOD LUCK

We started the book with a discussion about the classroom atmosphere and how you are the creator and controller of that atmosphere. Let's come full circle and remind ourselves how your mood is affected by the quality of your sleep, too. This job is not easy at the best of times, but a tired teacher has far less patience for their pupils than one who is refreshed and restored by the power of a good night's sleep.

Let's end by not forgetting that – at its best, when we are on top form and our students are in full flow – this is the most incredible job in the world. No government interference, no staffroom politics and no parent complaint can ever separate us from the reason we do what we do – the students. The children we work with are incredible, joyous and so very special. The fact that we get to have a small say in the type of person they go on to become in later life is a gift and a privilege very few other careers can offer.

Cast your mind back through the last 12 months you've had as a teacher. There is every chance you have laughed, you have cried, you may have grieved, you've wept with pride or lost sleep with worry over your students' welfare. There are children you have taught who you will never forget until the day you die and there are children who have challenged and frustrated you to the point at which you wonder why you even bother. At a time when teacher recruitment and retention is in crisis, you are still here on the front line and still doing everything you can to be the best teacher you can be for your pupils.

You do all of this because you care and it matters to you. And you know how I know this? You made it to the end of this book, which is all about making the lives of the children in your class better. You could have been playing on your phone, you could have been watching Netflix and you could have been taking a nap, but you didn't do that. You sacrificed those guilty pleasures to read about your job and to find ways in which you can do it better. That speaks volumes.

So, on behalf of all of those kids who are lucky to have you in their lives – thank you. I hope there is something you have taken from this little overview of wellbeing that helps you along the way. I wish you every success.

Jamie O'Dowd

MAPPING/VISUALISING WELLBEING INTERVENTIONS: THE SPEEDOMETER

It can be helpful to have a map or visual representation that outlines your school's approach to wellbeing interventions, to include formal and informal interventions. This example takes the form of a 'speedometer' and uses the 'RAG' (red, amber, green) rating to show the increase in severity or wellbeing need that results in further intervention.

This graphic also shows the range of data that is consulted to better understand each child's wellbeing, from the observable (uniform and attendance) to the quantitative data such as academic reports, PASS (Pupil Attitude to Self and School) data and CAT (Cognitive Abilities Tests) scores. When schools have a global overview that can be demonstrated visually in this way, it shows that there is a clear strategy and leadership of wellbeing which is transparent and accessible to all.

THE A–Z OF STUDENT WELLBEING

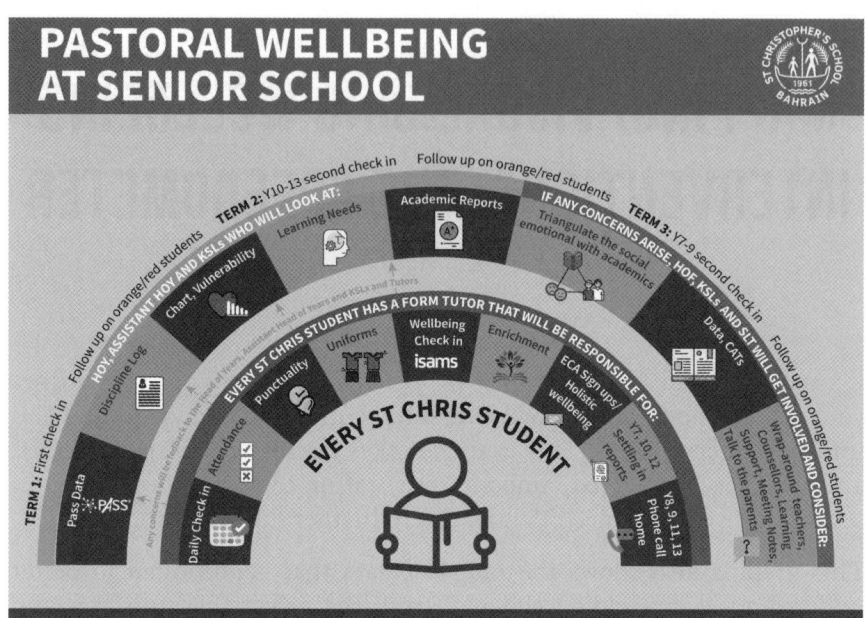

The 'speedometer' used to map wellbeing at St Christopher's School, Bahrain

DIGITAL LEADERSHIP FRAMEWORK

Schools, pastoral leaders and teachers are increasingly finding themselves policing not only their own schools and classrooms, but also the wild west of the online and digital worlds. Schools that value physical and emotional wellbeing also find a place to consider digital wellbeing.

Extending your school's policies to the online world can often result in you ending up in a swamp of many grey areas. How responsible is your school for bullying online when it has taken place out of school hours? What does your policy say, for example, about a fight that took place at the weekend, but that was filmed and shared among the community, in which the students were identifiable by the fact they wore their PE kit and the school's logo was clearly visible?

Children live two lives: their physical life and their digital life. Schools can choose to ignore the digital one, and leave that responsibility to the parents, or they can develop policies, systems and education to support children to live safely in both.

This image is an example of a digital framework used at St Christopher's School that contains eight distinct topic areas that are taught from Year 1 right through to Year 13. The six concepts around the edge of the graphic show the progression from simply being a digital citizen to the goal state on the far right where students become digital leaders. The 'Be...' statements in the middle all drill down into activities and learning exercises that allow the development of essential skills and knowledge to enable the learner to be proficient in that area.

This framework promotes positive wellbeing by ensuring that students have the skills and knowledge to be safe online and to contribute positively and responsibly in online and digital environments.

THE A–Z OF STUDENT WELLBEING

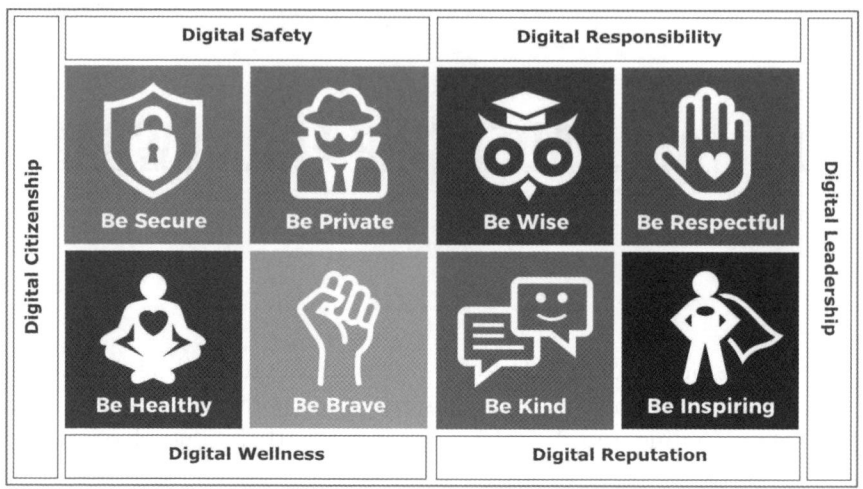

A digital leadership framework

AUDITING YOUR STAKEHOLDERS

3

In advance of any changes or improvements to your wellbeing provision, it is useful to consult your stakeholders to better understand their attitudes and beliefs around your current provision. Some simple questions that should be asked of all stakeholders are included below. These can be used to gain an overview of attitudes ahead of a deeper dive through focus groups and interviews. The responses to these questions should be collected using a Likert scale of 1–5.

QUESTIONS TO ASK TEACHING STAFF

To what extent are the majority of teachers in this school willing to teach wellbeing?
Are the majority of teachers in this school able to teach wellbeing?
To what extent does this school value student welfare and wellbeing above all else?
Is there a regular timetabled lesson where wellbeing/mental health is taught?
To what extent are teachers involved in the planning and delivery of these lessons?
Do teachers have time to prepare and personalise resources ahead of the lesson?
Do most teachers in this school enjoy working with children/young people?
Is there a named governor responsible for wellbeing/mental health in my school?

QUESTIONS TO ASK PARENTS

Is my child's happiness and wellbeing in school more important to me than their grades?
To what extent does this school value student welfare and wellbeing above all else?
Do I know what my child learns about wellbeing and mental health in school?
Is there someone to go to if I need to talk about my child's wellbeing or mental health?

QUESTIONS TO ASK STUDENTS

Do the teachers in this school teach wellbeing as well as they teach their subject?
Are wellbeing lessons relevant to my age?
Can what I learn in wellbeing lessons be used in real life?
Does this school value student welfare and wellbeing above all else?
Is there someone to go to if I need to talk about my wellbeing or mental health?

EXAMPLE LANGUAGE CHARTER 4

Language charters are most effective when they are created collectively to include all stakeholders. Parents, teachers and students should all contribute to the charter to ensure their needs are met according to the type of language they feel is most harmful or damaging in your school. Depending on your context, you may have different issues or sensitivities towards discriminatory language. Racism, sexism, homophobia, transphobia, islamophobia and language around gang culture, weapons, guns or knives may be highly relevant or completely irrelevant to your school.

This example from St Christopher's School gives you a flavour of how a language charter may be structured and worded to ensure it offers a positive reinforcement around acceptable and unacceptable language use in the school.

THE A–Z OF STUDENT WELLBEING

ST CHRIS LANGUAGE CHARTER
Senior School. 2023/24

At St Christopher's School we understand the power and impact of our words, in any language, spoken or written. In the spirit of inclusivity, kindness and respect, all staff and students need to be aware of the following:

We will not use language that discriminates against or disrespects any member of the school community according to their race, religion, gender, ethnicity, socio-economic status, physical appearance, mental wellness or disability.

-

We will not use offensive language, gestures, emojis, images, memes, accents or stereotypes that may be considered racist or have racist connotations, including microaggressions.

-

We take responsibility for the impact of our words when they have negatively impacted on another person or caused offence. We do not hide behind the excuse, 'it was a joke'.

-

We do not participate in online or in-person 'roasting', 'trolling' or similar behaviours which have the sole intent of passing judgement, causing distress, embarrassment or harm to another person.

-

We refrain from the sharing and spreading of allegations, rumours and gossip which may cause distress, embarrassment or harm to another person.

-

We do not use language that may be considered aggressive, threatening, confrontational or hostile. When resolving differences, we do so calmly and respectfully. Where needed, we ask an adult for support in resolving issues.

-

We will value all members of the St Chris community and beyond, upholding the core values of caring, honesty and mutual respect - our language reflects that.

© St Christopher's School

An example of a language charter

ENRICHMENT/RSE 'ROADMAP' {5}

Having a clear strategy and sequence for your wellbeing curriculum is essential. Teachers, pupils and parents need to be able to see that the content delivered in your allocated RSE time each week contributes to an overall plan that clearly develops and enhances the holistic development of the pupil.

Roadmaps have become very popular in teaching as a way of simplifying visually the journey that a learner will go through in a specific subject area. You can often find these in schools as displays in corridors and on notice boards.

Mapping out the sequence for RSE or enrichment should be no different from curriculum planning in any other subject area. This example shows how the topics covered increase in complexity and challenge as the students progress from Year 7 to Year 13. While the graphic does not go into granular detail, key wellbeing and mental health topics are embedded each year, with increasingly complex and mature subject matter appropriate to the ages of the students.

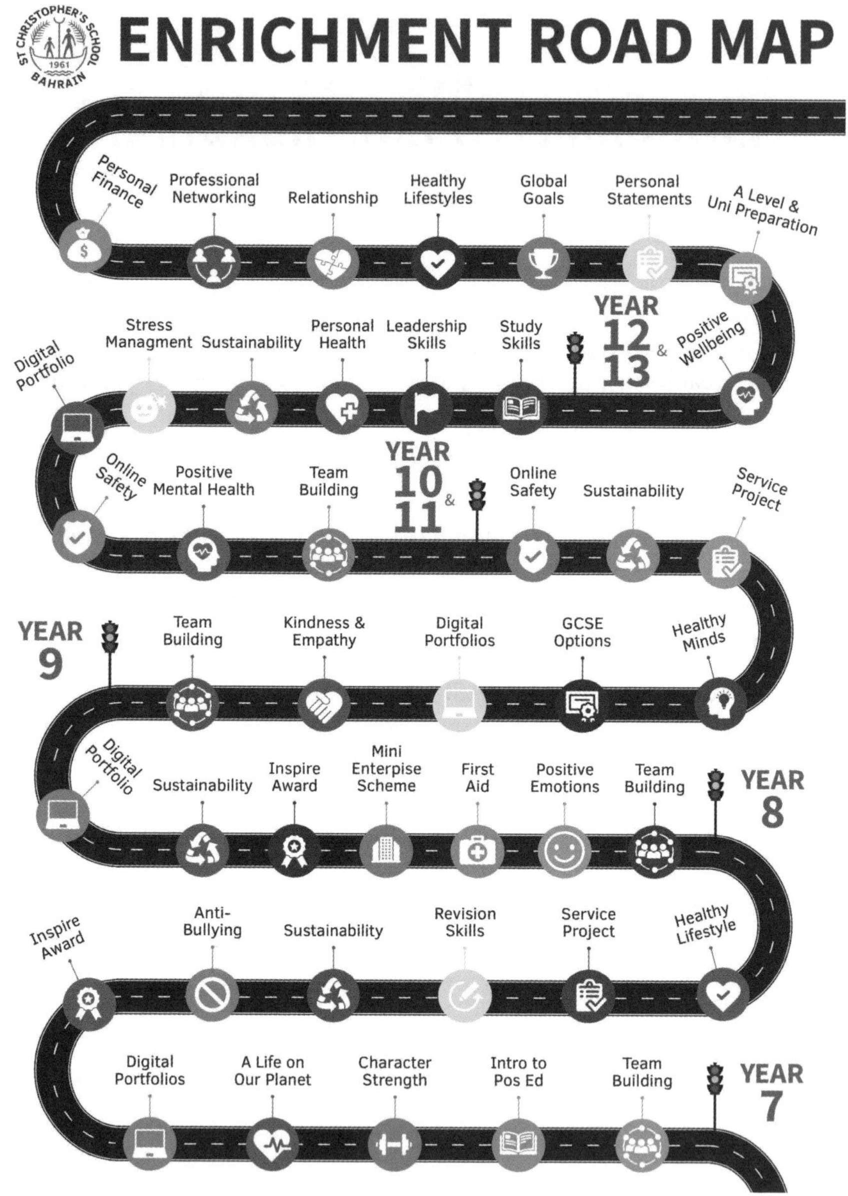

THE A–Z OF STUDENT WELLBEING

The enrichment 'roadmap' used at St Christopher's

SAFEGUARDING LEGISLATION AND POLICY

KEY HISTORIC AND CONTEMPORARY DOCUMENTS

1. **Children Act 1989 and 2004**: These Acts introduced the principle that the welfare of the child is paramount. They set out the duties of local authorities, courts, parents and other agencies in relation to the care and protection of children. The Children Act 2004 reinforced the 1989 Act and introduced the concept of 'Every Child Matters', which emphasised the importance of safeguarding children's welfare across all services following the death of Victoria Climbié in February 2000.

2. **Education Act 2002**: This Act places a statutory duty on schools and local authorities to safeguard and promote the welfare of children. Section 175 of the Act specifically requires local education authorities and the governing bodies of maintained schools and further education institutions to make arrangements for ensuring that their functions are carried out with a view to safeguarding and promoting the welfare of children.

3. **Working Together to Safeguard Children 2018**: This statutory guidance is a critical document that outlines how organisations and individuals should work together to safeguard and promote the welfare of children. It provides a framework for interagency cooperation and sets out the roles and responsibilities of different agencies, including schools, in safeguarding children.

4. **Keeping Children Safe in Education (KCSIE) 2015**: This is statutory guidance issued by the Department for Education for schools and colleges in England. It sets out the legal duties schools must follow to ensure they are safeguarding and promoting the

welfare of children. KCSIE is updated regularly and covers a wide range of issues, including the role of the DSL, staff training and the procedures for managing allegations of abuse against staff.

5. **The Safeguarding Vulnerable Groups Act 2006**: This Act led to the creation of the Disclosure and Barring Service (DBS), which helps prevent unsuitable individuals from working with children. Schools must ensure that all staff and volunteers undergo DBS checks to determine their suitability to work with children.

6. **The Children and Social Work Act 2017**: This Act introduced provisions to improve support for looked-after children and care leavers, promote the welfare and safeguarding of children, and establish the Child Safeguarding Practice Review Panel, which reviews serious child-safeguarding cases.

7. **Sexual Violence and Sexual Harassment Between Children in Schools and Colleges 2017**: This guidance, which supplements KCSIE, provides schools and colleges with advice on how to handle cases of sexual violence and sexual harassment between children. It emphasises the importance of creating a culture where such issues are not tolerated and are dealt with promptly and appropriately.

8. **The Prevent Duty (Counter-Terrorism and Security Act 2015)**: The Prevent Duty requires schools to have due regard to the need to prevent people from being drawn into terrorism. This includes safeguarding children from radicalisation and extremism by promoting British values, ensuring staff are trained to identify risks, and knowing how to report concerns.

9. **The Equality Act 2010**: This Act provides a legal framework to protect the rights of individuals and advance equality of opportunity. Schools must ensure that their safeguarding practices do not discriminate against any child on the basis of race, disability, gender, religion or any other protected characteristic.

10. **Data Protection Act 2018 and GDPR**: These laws govern how schools handle and protect personal data, ensuring that children's information is managed securely and used appropriately in safeguarding contexts.

MINDFULNESS SCRIPT

This is a script that guides teachers through a mindfulness activity known as 'body scan'. This helps children focus only on being present in their thoughts and feelings.

- Close your eyes. Let your shoulders drop down and away from your ears. Now, focus on your breathing. Take a slow breath in ... and out ... and just keep focusing on your breathing. The goal of this exercise is to just notice things happening in different parts of your body. Try not to get caught thinking about whether things in your body feel good, bad, uncomfortable or painful.
- Just see if you can notice what you feel – for example, do you notice tingling, warmth, tightness or something else. Again, it's not about whether these things feel good or bad, it's just about noticing them.
- Continue to breathe in ... and out .... Notice your lungs slowly filling up with air when you breathe in and slowly going down when you breathe out. Just like a balloon when you blow it up and then slowly let the air out.
- Now, focus on the parts of your body touching the floor, couch or chair. Every time you breathe out, let your body sink a little deeper into the surface below you.
- Focus on your left foot and notice what you feel. You don't need to do anything about those sensations, just notice them. Now focus on the bottom of your left leg or calf. Notice any sensations.
- You don't need to do anything about them, just let them be there. Now, focus on the upper part, or thigh, of your left leg. Whatever sensations you feel, just let them be there. If you don't feel anything at the moment, that's okay too.

- Now, focus on your right foot and leg. Simply notice all the feelings and sensations. Just notice. You don't need to do anything about them.
- Our minds will often wander off and we'll start thinking about other things. When you notice your mind has wandered, try to bring it back to your breath. Just focus on your breathing.
- Now focus on your stomach. Feel it rising as you breathe in. Sinking as you breathe out. Nice and slow. Keep breathing in ... and out.... Continue to notice any feelings or sensations in your stomach.
- Now focus on your left hand and left arm. Notice what you feel. Again, if you don't feel anything at the moment, that's okay.
- Now focus on your right hand and right arm. And just notice what you feel.
- Now focus on your chest, neck and face. Feel the sensations in your jaw and your throat. Notice how the back and the top of your head feel.
- Now, take a moment to notice your whole body and how every part is connected. Notice what you feel – tingling, warmth, coolness or heaviness. Notice what you feel without thinking about it as being good or bad, or that you have to do anything about it. Just notice.
- Now focus again on your breathing. Notice your lungs filling up and coming down as you breathe in and out. Keep focusing on your breathing and, when you are ready, slowly open your eyes.

REFERENCES

Al Taher, R. (2016). "Character Strengths & Virtues: The Classification Explained" *PositivePsychology.com* August 2016. Available at: https://positivepsychology.com/classification-character-strengths-virtues/

Doward, J. (2004). 'Television blamed for suicide rise'. *The Guardian*, 18 April. Available at: www.theguardian.com/media/2004/apr/18/broadcasting.mentalhealth

Dweck, C.S. (2016). *Mindset: The new psychology of success*. New York: Random House.

Luce, A. (2016). *The Bridgend Suicides: Suicide and the media*. London: Palgrave Macmillan.

Manuel, A. (2022). *Growing with Gratitude: Building resilience, happiness, and mental wellbeing in our schools and homes*. Richmond, Victoria: John Wiley & Sons, Australia.

NHS England (2023). 'Mental health of children and young people in England, 2023'. NHS, 21 November 2023. Available at: https://digital.nhs.uk/data-and-information/publications/statistical/mental-health-of-children-and-young-people-in-england/2023-wave-4-follow-up

Nottingham, J. (2017). *The Learning Challenge: How to guide your students through the learning pit to achieve deeper understanding*. Thousand Oaks, California: Corwin, a Sage company.

Peterson, C. & Seligman, M.E.P. (2004). *Character Strengths and Virtues: A handbook and classification*. Washington, DC, New York: American Psychological Association/Oxford University Press.

Sinek, S. (2011). *Start with Why: How great leaders inspire everyone to take action.* London: Penguin Books Ltd.

Seligman, M.E.P. (2002). *Authentic Happiness.* Boston: Nicholas Brealey Publishing.

Seligman, M.E.P. (2012). *Flourish.* New York: Simon & Schuster.

Tuckman, B.W. (1965). 'Developmental sequence in small groups'. *Psychological Bulletin.* 63, pp384–399.

United Nations (1990). 'Convention on the rights of the child'. Available at: www.ohchr.org/en/instruments-mechanisms/instruments/convention-rights-child

The A–Z series focuses on the 'fun and fundamentals' of what's happening in primary, special and secondary schools today. Each title is written by a leading practitioner, adopting a series approach of reflection, advice and provocation.

As a group of authors with a strong belief in the power of education to shape and change young people's lives, we hope teachers and leaders in the UK and internationally enjoy what we have to say.

Roy Blatchford, series editor

The A–Z of Great Classrooms (2023)
The A–Z of Secondary Leadership (2023)
The A–Z of Primary Maths (2024)
The A–Z of School Improvement (2024)
The A–Z of Diversity and Inclusion (2024)
The A–Z of Trust Leadership (2024)
The A–Z of International School Leadership (2024)
The A–Z of Special Educational Needs (2024)
The A–Z of Early Career Teaching (2024)
The A–Z of Student Wellbeing (2025)
The A–Z of Addressing Disadvantage (forthcoming)
The A–Z of Good Governance (forthcoming)
The A–Z of Primary Leadership (forthcoming)
The A–Z of Independent School Leadership (forthcoming)
The A–Z of Primary English (forthcoming)